I Ching
for **Beginners**

For more than twenty years, **Mark McElroy** designed training for MCI, Office Depot, Staples, and other major companies. Today, as the author of *Putting the Tarot to Work* and *Taking the Tarot to Heart,* he writes books and creates tools designed to help people lead more satisfying lives. For free tips on boosting creativity and achieving personal goals, visit Mark on the web at www.TarotTools.com.

I Ching
for Beginners

A Modern Interpretation
of the Ancient Oracle

Mark McElroy

Llewellyn Publications
Woodbury, Minnesota

First Edition
Third Printing, 2008

Book design and layout by Joanna Willis
Cover design by Gavin Dayton Duffy
Editing by Valerie Valentine

Llewellyn is a registered trademark of Llewellyn Worldwide, Ltd.

Library of Congress Cataloging-in-Publication Data
    I Ching for beginners: a modern interpretation of the ancient oracle / Mark McElroy.—1st ed.
        p.   cm.
    ISBN 13: 978-0-7387-0744-0
    ISBN 10: 0-7387-0744-9
    1. Divination—China. 2. Yi jing. I. Title.

BF1773.2.C5M39 2005
133.3'3—dc22

2005040945

Llewellyn Worldwide does not participate in, endorse, or have any authority or responsibility concerning private business transactions between our authors and the public.
    All mail addressed to the author is forwarded but the publisher cannot, unless specifically instructed by the author, give out an address or phone number.
    Any Internet references contained in this work are current at publication time, but the publisher cannot guarantee that a specific location will continue to be maintained. Please refer to the publisher's website for links to authors' websites and other sources.

Llewellyn Publications
A Division of Llewellyn Worldwide, Ltd.
2143 Wooddale Drive, Dept. 978-0-7387-0744-0
Woodbury, MN 55125-2989, U.S.A.
www.llewellyn.com

Printed in the United States of America

Other Books in the For Beginners Series

Astrology for Beginners
William W. Hewitt

Chakras for Beginners
David Pond

Divination for Beginners
Scott Cunningham

Healing Alternatives for Beginners
Kay Henrion

Magick for Beginners
J. H. Brennan

Meditation for Beginners
Stephanie Clement

Practical Magic for Beginners
Brandy Williams

Psychic Development for Beginners
William W. Hewitt

This one's for Amy,
who sings as beautifully as she smiles.

Contents

About This Book

I Ching for Beginners is neither a translation nor a paraphrase of the I Ching. Instead, this book contains a simplified oracle based on observations and insights taken from the Book of Changes.

The original text is a work of great beauty and depth. Contemporary readers, however, struggle with its obscure symbolism ("A man with purple rags tied around his knees approaches") and culturally bound metaphors (in one case, the I Ching illustrates the potential benefits of focused attention by pointing out how much better housewives behave when kept ignorant of the outside world).

This version attempts to relate the wisdom of the I Ching to contemporary life, and to express that wisdom in plain English. It strips away obscure references, freely updates metaphors and symbols, and recasts ancient ideas in everyday terms. It also adds features (questions, keywords, and applications) designed to help readers apply the advice they receive.

These actions have been taken with great deliberation and intend no disrespect.

Acknowledgments

Carl, Sandra, and Gabe Weschcke continue to attract some of the industry's most capable and imaginative people to Llewellyn—thank you for your vision, your wisdom, and your faith in my work. Thanks, too, to the entire sales staff, who have been tireless in their efforts to get this book on shelves all over the world.

Valerie Valentine, New Submissions Editor, kept me updated and informed throughout the project . . . and made excellent suggestions for expanding and enhancing the "how to" chapters. Thanks go to Karl Anderson for stepping into the editorial role at the last minute and making important changes prior to publication. Thanks, too, to Gavin Duffy for his work on the cover art.

I must also thank Barbara Moore for her enthusiasm and patience; again and again, Barbara, you delight me with your professionalism and good, common sense.

Since Chinese is all Greek to me, I'm indebted to the numerous authors and scholars who have penned approachable, scholarly translations of the I Ching: Jack Balkin, Robert Benson, Sarah Dening, Richard Wilhelm, Cary F. Baynes, and especially Steven Karcher.

And finally: years ago, I watched an elderly Chinese woman practicing divination. Standing in the freezing cold, she bowed her head, concentrated, and shook a bamboo canister until one of the several numbered sticks fell to the floor.

I do not know her name, and I do not know the answer she received. But that image—her earnest face, her intense concentration, the sight of the divinatory stick falling to the floor—was the catalyst for all my research into divination. Since that moment, nothing has been quite the same.

Whoever you are, wherever you are . . . I offer you my sincere thanks.

Introduction

Note: This introduction is intended for thoughtful types who want to know something about a tool before they turn it on. If you're feeling twitchy, if you're in a hurry for help, or if you don't care where the I Ching came from or how it works, skip this introduction and go directly to the next section: "Consulting the I Ching: Step by Step." (You can always come back later.)

Otherwise . . . stick around! Spend fifteen minutes reading this chapter, and you'll get much more out of your work with the oracle.

Turn, Turn, Turn

What goes around, comes around. After the darkness comes the dawn. What goes up, must come down. One thing leads to another. The more things change, the more they stay the same. There's nothing new under the sun.

These familiar quotes testify to a fact of human existence: life consists of a series of cycles. In politics, we go from liberal to conservative and back again. You finally throw away those embarrassing bell bottom jeans from high school days, and twenty-four hours later, bell bottoms become the hottest "new" fashion trend.

As innocence gives way to experience (that's my nice way of saying, "As we get older . . ."), we increasingly experience déjà vu. When our boss says, "I really can't say whether anyone in our department will be laid off or not," we know what's coming. When our daughter mentions how much she likes the neighbor boy's full-body tattoos, we know what's coming. When we tell ourselves, "Okay, this time, I'm sticking to my diet *no matter what!*" . . . well, you get the idea.

Over time, we become aware of life's patterns. In the tiny details of day-to-day existence, we see the seeds of what's coming next. We understand how one event gives rise to another.

If you can pile up this much insight in a single lifetime, imagine how much insight you could rack up over thirty-five hundred years!

Know What's Coming, Know What to Do

That's about how long a remarkable book, called the *I Ching*, has been around, give or take a few centuries. The *I Ching* contains a series of chapters describing *every possible life situation*. In addition to describing everything that *can* happen to you, the I Ching also offers, based on thousands of years of observation, extremely specific descriptions of what is most likely to happen next.

How can a Chinese book written thirty-five hundred years ago anticipate every situation in modern life? Good question. After all, we're living in the twenty-first century. We've got the Internet. We've got mobile phones that transmit live video. We've got break-and-bake cookie dough *and* great-tasting diet sodas sweetened with Splenda.

Remember what we said at the beginning of the chapter? *The more things change, the more they stay the same.* The players change, but the roles they play—father, mother, brother, sister, friend, lover, patron, enemy, employer— have been around since humanity first appeared. Centuries ago, the party invitations I now handle with wireless email would have been written on parchment, but the goal—getting people together to celebrate a victory—is as old as mankind. Times change, but motivations (greed, anger, love, passion, jealousy, shame, joy, patriotism) are eternal.

So, despite its age (and, perhaps, *due* to its age), the I Ching continues to make relevant observations and offer accurate predictions. For centuries, emperors and kings have depended on its counsel. Generals have modified battle plans based on its feedback. Today, the I Ching continues to shape the consciousness—and fate—of one of the planet's oldest and most vibrant civilizations.

With *I Ching for Beginners* in hand, you have everything you need to start exploring the wisdom and power of this book for yourself. If you approach this study with a combination of reverence and a spirit of adventure, you'll soon discover the two benefits that make the I Ching unique among books of ancient wisdom:

1. The I Ching tells you, no matter what the situation, what is most likely to happen next, and

2. The I Ching tells you, very specifically, what you can do to best take advantage of the situation as it evolves.

Common Mythconceptions

Given the remarkable potential of such a book, you'd think everyone would know about the I Ching.

Strangely, while we live in a time when your Great Aunt Mabel practices *feng shui* and Madonna's made *Kaballah* a household word, almost no one's heard of the I Ching. (Example: when I told my mother I was writing *I Ching for Beginners*, she thought I was compiling a collection of quick and easy noodle dishes.)

If you know the following facts, you'll know more about the I Ching than 99 percent of the people you meet. That won't make you an I Ching expert—some people have devoted their entire lives to studying the book—but you will be able to explain clearly to your friends what the book is, and what benefits it offers.

Some Say Tomato . . .

Some people say *eee ching*. Others say *yee jing*. Pick one of these pronunciations and stick to it. Don't say "*eye* ching," though; when you do, folks in the know will grin.

If foreign words make you nervous, it's perfectly okay to use the English title: *Book of Changes.*

Tso Who Wrote It . . . and Wen?

Tradition teaches that a wise and powerful Chinese ruler, King Wen, contributed to the first draft of the Book of Changes about thirty-five hundred years ago.

Chinese tradition, though, frequently credits great discoveries to great leaders, whether or not those leaders were directly involved. Ever ordered General Tso's Chicken from your local Chinese restaurant? General Tso, a well-liked military leader from the 1800s, probably never tasted the dish. Those spicy, deep-fried nuggets of saucy poultry were probably named in tribute to the General; it's possible, for similar reasons, that the I Ching was merely attributed to King Wen.

It's also good to know that, over time, the text of the Book of Changes has been refined, edited, and expanded.

Huge commentaries—some apparently written by the great philosopher Confucius himself—have been appended to the I Ching.

The material in the commentaries provides detailed, scholarly analysis of each and every line of the book. If you're curious about these, you've got an entire lifetime to look them up! To keep things simple, *I Ching for Beginners* focuses exclusively on the sixty-four passages devoted to mapping change and determining what will happen next.

Fortunately, More than Fortune Telling

While you *can* tell fortunes with the I Ching, doing so is a bit like using a fancy plasma screen television as a doorstop—it works, but you aren't really getting what you paid for.

For centuries, the I Ching has been regarded as a powerful tool for *divination*—the art of tapping into the Divine Will, often by assigning meaning to an apparently random arrangement of objects or events. The ultimate goal? Bringing your life into alignment with the Will of God (or the Goddess, or the universe, or your higher power . . . you get the idea) by taking the best possible actions at the best possible time.

By aligning ourselves as closely as possible with the Divine Plan—also called the *tao* (pronounced "dow") or "The Way"—we greatly improve our chances for happiness and success. By contrast, fortune telling does little more than attempt to foresee future events. Fortune tellers usually assume the future is unavoidable—the metaphysical equivalent of a Mack truck headed in your direction. Not very empowering, eh?

The practice of divination goes way beyond fortune telling. Fortune tellers ask, "What will happen?" Someone working with the I Ching asks, "Given what I want to happen . . . and given what's likely to happen . . . what course of action keeps me closest to my own best possible path?"

No Faith? No Problem.

For just a moment, let's pretend we never mentioned divination. Let's put aside all metaphysics and "New Age mumbo jumbo." Let's pretend the world exclusively exists of what we can see, touch, and measure. (Scary thought, eh?)

Even in such a sterile environment, the I Ching still has much to recommend it:

Consulting the book provides an opportunity for reflection. All too often, in the rush to take action, we fail to invest ten or twenty minutes in quiet reflection. What's the higher purpose of our effort? What's the goal? What's Plan B? Consulting the I Ching provides an opportunity to see our questions or situations from an alternative, more objective point of view.

Consulting the book encourages awareness of impact.
Even as it enhances our perspective, the book's emphasis
on "What happens next?" encourages us to envision outcomes . . . *before* we take action. Ever bought a shiny new
doodad, only to regret the purchase later? You can maximize success and minimize regret by consulting the Book
of Changes first.

Consulting the book moderates our responses. Impulsive?
The I Ching frequently recommends a "wait and see" approach. Inclined to let opportunity pass you by? The Book
of Changes doesn't hesitate to deliver a friendly "kick in
the pants." The stability of Chinese culture over the centuries has been attributed, at least in part, to this book's
moderating influence. Again and again, the book steers
readers away from extremes and closer to middle ground.

**Consulting the book is like getting advice from an expe-
rienced friend.** The I Ching has survived, in part, because
its recommendations make sense. When you work with the
book, you'll hear the simple wisdom of its voice—the balanced, gentle tone of someone who's been there, done
that, and gotten the T-shirt to prove it. Used properly, the
I Ching offers frank, straightforward advice informed by
thousands of years of experience and wisdom. What you
do with that advice, of course, is always up to you.

Working with the Book of Changes

When you're reading *Inspector Clueless and The Murder at Millhouse Mansion*, skipping around in the book is strongly discouraged. Mysteries—like most books—are written with cover-to-cover reading in mind.

Unlike other books, the I Ching is not meant to be read from beginning to end. We'll cover the details later, but for now, here's an overview of how to consult the I Ching:

Step One: Come up with a question.

Take some time with this, because the more specific the question, the more specific the answer. Questions that begin with the words "How can I?" or "What should I do about?" are particularly easy to work with. (You can always ask a yes or no question . . . but at that rate, why not just flip a coin?)

Step Two: Find the passage that "speaks" to you.

Having defined your question, find the associated passage in the text of the I Ching. There are several time-honored methods for doing this:

Method One: Self-Service

Once they become familiar with the Book of Changes, many people flip directly to the chapter that deals with their situation. If going through a rough patch, for example, they might turn to Chapter 36, "Surviving Dark Times."

Attaining that degree of familiarity with the I Ching (and achieving the necessary degree of objectivity!) could take decades. As a result, it's far more common (and a lot more fun) to be guided to the best passage through the process of divination.

Method Two: Divination

As you'll recall from earlier in this chapter, divination attempts to tap into the Divine Will by assigning meaning to apparently random events.

Pay careful attention to the phrase *apparently random*, because two of the chief assumptions underlying divination are:

1. There are no accidents; all events are infused with design and meaning.

2. All objects and events are connected to, reflect, and influence each other.

With these assumptions in place, any *apparently* random arrangement of objects—sticks, coins, stones, or tarot cards—cannot be regarded as merely accidental. Instead, the patterns they create amount to *a random sample of all events and influences at work in the moment*. Psychologist Carl Jung coined a term to describe this principle: *synchronicity*, or "meaningful coincidence."

What does all that mean in plain English? Simply this: when you roll dice, toss coins, shake sticks, deal cards, or perform any random act, what happens isn't really random at all. Because all events connect with, reflect, and influence each other, those scattered coins on the floor aren't a mess—they're a message!

Several popular methods exist for "entering the moment" through divination:

Point and Shoot. It doesn't get much easier than this: open the book, flip through its pages, and select a passage at random. Talk about the fickle finger of fate! People who favor this method believe a combination of intuition and synchronicity leads them to the exact passage they need to discover at the time.

The Sixty-Four Card Shuffle. The I Ching contains sixty-four chapters; many people take sixty-four numbered cards (often, one of the several specialized I Ching card decks now available), shuffle them, pull one, and then flip to the associated chapter. Don't want to buy a card deck? Scratch the numbers one through sixty-four onto poker chips and toss 'em in a bag.

Stick with Tradition. One of the oldest methods for consulting the I Ching is to use bundles of foot-long sticks, which are tossed, sorted, and counted. This complex process generates a series of numbers indicating which chapter of the Book of Changes applies to your question. (Since this method is complex and time consuming—and since most people don't have forty-nine foot-long sticks handy—we won't cover it in *I Ching for Beginners*.)

Coin a Phrase. By tossing three identical coins, you can quickly and easily generate numbers that refer you to an appropriate I Ching passage. Any three identical coins will do, as long as they have "heads" and "tails." Step-by-step instructions for this method—which, despite its simplicity, still requires some basic math skills—are provided in the next chapter.

Flash Cards. If you're a math-a-phobe like me, you'll appreciate the simplicity of this card-based method, which I created as a way to avoid noodling over numbers. Details are in the next chapter . . . for now, just know that with sixteen index cards and a magic marker, you'll be good to go!

Step Three: Apply the Wisdom

Having asked a question and received an answer, now the fun begins: applying the passage to your specific situation.

I Ching for Beginners makes relating the book's advice to your specific situation easier than ever by providing:

- An easy-to-understand title for each chapter
- A poetic, one- or two-line summary of the message of the chapter, especially designed for folks with short attention spans

- Keywords designed to help you brainstorm connections between your question and the passage itself
- Brief paragraphs describing what the chapter encourages and warns against
- A list of questions designed to help you explore the message of the chapter in terms of your own experience
- Clear, plain-English readings inspired by the original text of the I Ching. In addition to general advice, you'll also find specific advice for relationship and work-related questions.

I Ching for Beginners is designed to make applying the wisdom found in the Book of Changes faster and easier than ever before. As you become more experienced, you may eventually wish to work with more traditional or scholarly translations; for now, though, this book provides everything you need.

How the Book of Changes Works

Enough tire-kicking! It's time to get under the hood of the Book of Changes and get a peek at its thirty-five hundred year-old Wisdom Engine: an ingenious problem-solving computer built back when the Silicon Valley was just the Silicon Gully.

The Eternal Dance of Yin and Yang

By now, everyone's heard of *yin* and *yang*—two principles Chinese philosophers believed blended together in various degrees to form the Tao, the "master pattern" of the universe. Yin, or the "feminine" principle, corresponds to femininity, receptivity, submissiveness, coolness, darkness, the earth, et cetera. Yang, or the "masculine" principle, relates to masculinity, creation, activity, aggression, light, heat, heaven, and so on.

Everything in the universe, including everything that happens, arises out of interaction between yin and yang. The I Ching symbolizes the yin (receptive) force with a broken line:

━ ━

The yang (active) force is symbolized by a solid, unbroken line:

━━━

If the universe existed of pure yin and pure yang, we could answer any question by flipping a coin! As you know, though, life is much more complicated than that.

Three Cheers for Trigrams

To represent a greater degree of complexity, the Chinese came up with *trigrams*: three lines stacked on top of each other, representing various mixtures of yin and yang. (Your Aunt Mabel will recognize these trigrams as the funny little symbols printed on the eight edges of her feng shui compass.) The trigrams are:

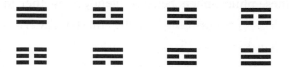

Philosophers associated all kinds of ideas with these trigrams, and they do allow for a more sophisticated look at the interplay of yin and yang. Even your cute little two-month-old nephew, though, has already lived through more than eight unique situations!

Heavy-Duty Hexagrams

When you see the first three letters of the word, you might think *hexagrams* are a unit for measuring the power of evil spells. Actually, hexagrams have nothing to do with that kind of hex; instead, a hexagram consists of six lines—an upper trigram and a lower trigram.

If you use divination to interact with the I Ching, the sixty-four hexagrams (representing all of the unique, six-line combinations of yin and yang possible) will become very familiar. Why? Because the main text of the I Ching consists of sixty-four chapters: one for each hexagram.

Almost all the methods of divination described earlier—particularly the ones using sticks, stones, and coins—are designed to do one thing: build a hexagram from the ground up. Each time you cast the coins or draw a stone, you get the information needed to draw one line of the hexagram, beginning with the bottom line. Cast the coins or draw a card six times, and voilà: a hexagram appears.

To find the chapter of the Book of Changes that comments on your situation, just match the hexagram to one of the sixty-four corresponding chapters of the I Ching. (The table in Appendix A makes this quick and easy.)

"But wait!" you say. "Sixty-four hexagrams can clearly say more than eight little trigrams. But I can tell you—without consulting *any* ancient Chinese book—that I've lived through more than sixty-four different situations!"

And so you have . . . which brings us to the most innovative feature of the I Ching: the *changing lines.*

Change for the Better

As it turns out, the I Ching is called the Book of Changes for good reason.

Fact is, we're very rarely in a static situation. The world doesn't stand still; by the time we perceive a moment, that moment is on the verge of changing into the next.

The I Ching handles this by incorporating changing lines—lines which are yin, but about to be yang . . . or lines that are yang, but about to be yin. The two kinds of changing lines are represented by special characters:

As you build a hexagram from scratch, some lines will be stable (represented by a simple solid or broken line). Some lines, however, will likely be changing (represented by the lines with the X and the O in the middles). These lines represent the aspects of your situation that are "in motion."

This innovation builds enormous flexibility into the system, giving the I Ching its remarkable ability to reflect the complexities of life.

For example: using one of the methods described in the next chapter, you generate the following hexagram:

This hexagram, with its three stable yin lines and three stable yang lines, describes a static, unchanging situation. If you received this hexagram, you would look up the corresponding chapter (Chapter 12—Falling Apart), apply the readings to your situation, and hunker down . . . because things won't be changing anytime soon!

Now, take a look at this hexagram:

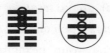

This is the same hexagram as before . . . but the top three lines are changing lines: considered solid for now, but on the verge of breaking.

Interpreting this hexagram requires three simple steps:

Step One: Look up the *primary hexagram*—the hexagram as it would appear if you ignored all potential for change. This hexagram would have three broken lines on the bottom and three solid lines at the top:

Using the table in Appendix A, you would identify this as Hexagram 12. Look up the associated chapter (Chapter 12—Falling Apart), and choose the most appropriate reading (General, Love & Relationships, or Work & Projects).

Step Two: Look up the commentary for any changing lines. In addition to the overall reading, each chapter offers additional advice for each one of the changing lines in your hexagram.

In this case, lines 4, 5, and 6 are all changing lines. For additional insight into your situation, you would read the changing lines entries for lines 4, 5, and 6.

Step Three: Look up the *secondary hexagram*—the hexagram as it appears when all lines have changed. This requires redrawing your hexagram with the changes complete:

Talk about useful information! Here, the changing lines indicate that your current situation, "Falling Apart" (Chapter 12), is changing into a situation in which "Being Receptive" (Chapter 2) will be your best possible option!

In addition to the primary commentary offered by the primary hexagram, changing lines provide you with situation-specific insights, offer a glimpse of the most likely outcome, and suggest a strategy for dealing effectively with what's still to come.

Note: Changing line commentaries are only read and applied to the primary hexagram. When looking up the secondary hexagram, ignore them.

What's Next?

Approached reverently and consulted with care, the I Ching will provide you with dependable advice. Having the Book of Changes on hand is like having access to a wise friend's counsel twenty-four hours a day, seven days a week.

Keep a level head, embrace your responsibility for making your own choices, and apply the book's wisdom according to your own best judgment. For all its wisdom and experience, the I Ching offers advice, not prescriptions! If your work with this book empowers you, you're on the right track.

So what are you waiting for? Turn to the next chapter, follow the simple step-by-step instructions, and begin your personal exploration of the Book of Changes!

Consulting the I Ching: Step by Step

This chapter begins with a quick overview of the various methods for consulting the Book of Changes. If you're in a hurry, feel free to skip to the section titled, "How to Consult the I Ching." Otherwise, please read on: the information in this chapter can greatly enrich your use of the oracle!

Sticks and Stones . . . and Coins, too!

One very early method for consulting the Book of Changes involved tossing and counting bundles of foot-long sticks. Some scholars think the process was deliberately designed to be complex and time-consuming—a sort of "spiritual speed bump" designed to force a more mindful approach and discourage casual use of the oracle.

But people—especially people with urgent questions on their minds—tend to be impatient. It's a good thing, then, that sometime during the twelfth or thirteenth centuries, a new method of consulting the oracle became popular: tossing three coins.

Both methods generate a hexagram—one of the sixty-four figures associated with each of the I Ching's divinatory passages. And while both methods are considered ancient and authentic, the coin-toss method (outlined in this chapter) has real advantages over the yarrow-stick method. First, coin tossing requires less counting. Second, it generates hexagrams faster. And finally, which are you more likely to have in your pocket: three coins . . . or fifty twelve-inch sticks?

There is a small trade-off involved. The individual lines—especially the number and frequency of changing lines—generated by the coin-based method differ somewhat from those produced by the yarrow-stick method. (It's a math thing.) For centuries, though, the convenience and speed of the coin-toss method has won out over the mathematical precision of the yarrow-stick method. The result? Long ago—hundreds of years ago, in fact—the three-coin method became the most popular means of consulting the oracle.

In his book, *I Ching: The Classic Chinese Oracle of Change* (Vega, 2002), Stephen Karcher suggests a new way to consult the oracle using sixteen colored tokens, marbles, or stones: one of one color, three of another color, five of another, and seven of yet another. Karcher places all these stones in a bag, shakes them up, and draws one at random. The color of the stone produced indicates the type of line to be drawn; after drawing the appropriate line, the consultant drops the stone back into the bag and repeats the process five more times.

This approach works quickly, avoids all counting, and eliminates the clatter associated with throwing three coins across a desk. In addition, because this method replicates the mathematical odds associated with the old yarrow stick method, it provides a faster way of consulting the oracle . . . without sacrificing precision.

Even the "stones in a bag" method, though, has a downside. As stones are drawn, consultants must constantly refer to a chart detailing which color stone corresponds to which type of line. Inexperienced consultants easily get confused, forgetting which colors respond to a given type of line. ("Did I say I'd make the *blue* stones represent stable yang . . . or the *red* ones? *D'oh!*")

For *I Ching for Beginners*, I've taken Karcher's method a step further, completely eliminating the need for any counting, charts, association, or memorization. In lieu of sixteen stones, I suggest you construct a simple deck of sixteen cards:

Make This Many Cards	*Featuring This Symbol*
1	━x━
3	━⊖━
5	━━━
7	━ ━

To consult the oracle and build a hexagram:

1. Shuffle the deck

2. Draw a card

3. Record the type of line you see on the card

4. Replace the card in the deck

5. Repeat the process until your hexagram is complete.

So: when consulting the oracle, should you use sticks, coins, stones, or cards? Your answer may well be dictated by comfort, convenience, or mathematical skill. In my work with the Book of Changes, I've used all these methods . . . and each time, regardless of method, I've received helpful insights and reassuring answers.

How to Consult the I Ching

What You Need

- A pen or pencil

- A sheet of paper

- *One* of the following:

Three identical coins. Antique Chinese coins are inexpensive, easy to find, and fun to use. In a pinch, quarters (or any coin with "heads" and "tails") do nicely.

Or

Sixteen index cards. To reduce the amount of math and table-checking involved in consulting the I Ching, you may wish to build the simple, handmade deck of 3 x 5 "consultation cards" I described earlier in this chapter.

Step One: Prepare for the Reading

1. If possible, find a quiet place. Take a few deep breaths. Slow down. Concentrate.

2. Consider your question carefully. While yes/no questions are welcome, questions beginning with "How can I" or "What can I" may prove more illuminating.

3. When you question is as clear and specific as you can make it, write it down.

Step Two: Generate the Hexagram

Note: when working with the I Ching, always build your hexagrams "from the ground, up." The first line is the bottom line . . . the second line goes above it . . . and so on, until you generate the sixth (top) line.

If Working with Coins

1. Gather the three coins.

2. Toss all three.

3. Refer to the table below to determine the type of line generated:

These Coin-Toss Results	Produce This Kind of Line
Three Heads	➖⊖➖
1 Head / 2 Tails	━━━
2 Heads / 1 Tail	▬ ▬
Three Tails	▬✕▬

4. Draw the line indicated.

Repeat this process six times.

If Working with Cards

1. Shuffle your deck.

2. Draw one card.

3. Draw the line indicated.

4. Return the card to the deck.

Repeat this process five more times.

Step Three: Interpret Changing Lines

If the resulting hexagram contains changing lines like these:

then your reading has generated two different hexagrams: one illustrating the present (the "primary" hexagram), and one indicating how the situation is most likely to unfold (the "secondary" hexagram).

To interpret your reading correctly:

Based on the hexagram you just created, draw the primary hexagram by referring to the table below:

Type of Line Received	*Primary Hexagram Line*

Next, draw the secondary hexagram by referring to the table below:

Type of Line Received	*Secondary Hexagram Line*

Example

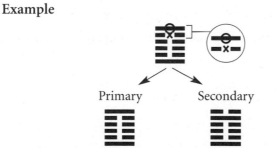

Primary   Secondary

HEXAGRAM 27   HEXAGRAM 3

If your original hexagram contains no changing lines, your situation is remarkably stable, and no secondary hexagram is needed.

Step Four: Receive Your Advice

1. Using the table in Appendix A, determine which chapter of the I Ching your hexagram corresponds to.

2. Look up the indicated chapter.

3. Read the chapter title, the At-a-Glance summary, the keywords, the paragraphs describing what this chapter encourages and warns against, the exploration questions, and the most appropriate reading (General, Love & Relationships, or Work & Projects).

If your hexagram *does not* contain changing lines, the reading ends here.

If your hexagram *does* contain changing lines, the presence of specific changes on specific lines of your hexagram yields additional insights and very specific advice.

4. For each changing line, check the Guide to Changing Lines. The additional advice applies *if and only if* the type of changing line indicated appears on the associated line of your hexagram.

5. After reading the Guide to Changing Lines, use the table in Appendix A to identify the chapter associated with your secondary hexagram.

6. Look up the indicated chapter, which will describe how your situation is evolving.

7. Read the chapter title, the At-a-Glance summary, the keywords, the paragraphs describing what this chapter encourages and warns against, the exploration questions, and the most appropriate reading (General, Love & Relationships, or Work & Projects).

Do not read any information under the Guide to Changing Lines.

Step Four: Meditate on the Meaning

Invest several minutes considering the advice you've received. Consider how you can tailor your approach to best align yourself with the situation as it evolved.

You may want to end your session with a few minutes of silence, a short prayer, or an expression of honor or gratitude.

The
TEXT
of the
ORACLE

1

Taking Action

Just as the sky changes constantly, an empowered person always works to become stronger.

Keywords: Decisive action, overwhelming strength, forceful motion, dynamic creativity, making a difference

Encourages: Taking decisive, appropriate action at the best possible time as a means of aligning yourself with the best possible future; setting priorities; focusing on the completion of fewer goals; being persistent; enhancing success by involving others

Cautions against: Charging ahead, wielding blind force, and pursuing your goals to the disadvantage of others; squandering energy by trying to do everything at once; being offensively forceful

THOUGHT QUESTIONS

To what extent have I set clear goals and priorities for myself?

Which goals are most important to me?

What steps or actions are absolutely essential to reaching my goal?

How can I move ahead in a way that encourages others to do the same?

Commentary

You are like a person climbing six great steps. Move too quickly, and you will exhaust yourself. Move too slowly, and you will never reach the summit. Move with determination and purpose, and your success is assured.

Natural forces, like rain and wind, shape the world . . . but they do so in accordance with natural law. Your actions should work this way, too: giving form to what you desire, but doing so in a way that is constructive, not destructive. Do the right thing at the right time.

Love & Relationships

A relationship can't be forced or manufactured, but doing the right thing at the right time can make all the difference in how someone feels. Move forward . . . but be attuned to the natural rhythm of the situation. In your heart, you know what to do, and how to do it.

Work & Projects

This is the right time to make progress . . . but, in doing so, be sure you've involved the people around you, or you may find yourself leading the charge to a lonesome destination. List the steps that must be taken, then take honorable, appropriate action.

Guide to Changing Lines

on the First Line

This is a time to gather your strength. Your time is near, but it isn't quite time to move ahead. Watch and wait. You'll know when the time is right.

on the Second Line

Your good position can be enhanced by getting good help. Calling on a trusted advisor or a capable colleague will make all the difference in your degree of success.

on the Third Line

Options and opportunities abound. If you pursue them all, you'll never achieve your primary goals. Cut away what isn't essential. Say no when you need to.

on the Fourth Line

You can move forward, or you can wait patiently. Neither course of action is right or wrong if the one you choose is in keeping with maintaining with your truest character.

━●━ *on the Fifth Line*

This is your time! Take the sort of action that will inspire others and win their approval. Be honorable in what you do, and the sky's the limit.

━●━ *on the Sixth Line*

Remember Icarus? Fly too high too quickly, and you'll set yourself up for a fall. Step back. Reexamine your motives and direction in order to avoid getting burned.

━●━ *on All Lines*

Forces in your situation are perfectly balanced, and this time is extremely favorable for you. Take appropriate action, and your degree of success may surprise even you.

2

Being Receptive

As a gentle mare submits to the reins, even an empowered person submits to leadership when appropriate.

Keywords: Waiting, reflecting, accepting, obeying, intuition, thoughtfulness, considering, tireless patience, responding wisely

Encourages: Practicing patience; pausing to listen to your feelings; being guided by others; understanding that sometimes following is the best way to lead

Cautions against: Being a doormat; following orders without question; accepting the leadership of unworthy people; manipulating others; a "pack" mentality

THOUGHT QUESTIONS

What does your intuition tell you about this situation?

How do you feel about following as opposed to leading?

When might sitting still be as difficult (and profitable) as doing something?

How can you identify a leader worthy of your support?

Commentary

Self-restraint requires just as much power as self-direction. A wise person knows this, and he scales his reaction to events with this principle in mind. When the direction and timing are right, allow yourself to be led. Do this, and success is assured.

Follow the example of the earth, which receives seeds and produces fruit. As events unfold around you, receive them . . . and by doing so, expand yourself and your awareness. Try responding instead of reacting; try following instead of leading.

Love & Relationships

In a world focused on "doing something," we often overlook the power of simply "being" with someone. You don't always have to be in control. Sometimes, going with the flow is the best option. Master the art of allowing others to make choices and set direction.

Work & Projects

There's a time to lead and a time to be just another member of the team. Supporting a project can be just as important and beneficial as guiding it. Enhance success by thinking and researching before taking timely action.

Guide to Changing Lines

━x━ *on the First Line*

A wise person avoids big problems by noticing when small things are going wrong. For now, take no action . . . but move quickly to correct small problems as they occur.

━x━ *on the Second Line*

Instead of exaggerating your qualities or acting like someone else, just be who you are. Work honestly, watch for what the situation calls for, and provide it as best you can.

━x━ *on the Third Line*

Forgo the spotlight. You don't have to be the center of attention in order to make a contribution. Fulfilling your responsibilities is enough for now.

━x━ *on the Fourth Line*

This situation is swirling with potential for confrontation. Exercise restraint. Keep your ideas, thoughts, and feelings to yourself for now.

▬x▬ *on the Fifth Line*

Moderate your responses with sincerity and sensitivity. Rather than impressing others with your insight, earn respect through quiet collaboration and support.

▬x▬ *on the Sixth Line*

Insure success by "sticking with it." Whatever happens, keep moving toward the goal. Become a stronger person by moving ahead, despite the obstacles.

Getting Started

The empowered person knows even a tiny blade of grass is strong enough to break through the earth.

Keywords: Initial resistance, gathering resources, difficulty, rocky start, being prepared, making ready

Encourages: Abandoning assumptions and finding facts; drawing up a realistic plan; gathering the resources and assistance needed in order to meet a goal; tapping into reserves; getting underway even when things aren't perfect

Cautions against: Waiting for someone else to do all the work; depending on others to the extent you debilitate yourself; forging ahead without acknowledging what you don't know or don't yet have; waiting for all obstacles to be removed before beginning

THOUGHT QUESTIONS

What information is being suppressed or overlooked?

What assumptions are you making? How can you identify and move beyond them?

What resources do you need? What research needs to be done?

To what extent have you defined contingencies? What's Plan B? Plan C? Plan Z?

Commentary

The first step in untying a complicated knot is identifying the role played by each individual thread. Your situation is complex, but careful attention to detail can help you resolve it. Yanking threads at random will only make things worse.

It's natural to feel unsettled or confused when undertaking something new. Calling on others may uncover the expertise needed to transform chaos into focus. Enhance chances for success by getting resources in order . . . and seeking sound, experienced advice.

Love & Relationships

There's goodness in having friends to rely on. Whatever the situation, draw on the counsel of those you most admire . . . or someone you know who has been here before.

Admitting you don't know what to do is often the first step toward resolving a problem.

Work & Projects

Don't hide your need for assistance. Pull in consultants or collaborators, and don't be afraid to drop your guard and ask questions. Rather than give in to pressure to plow ahead without a plan, insist on a project plan that defines what you need and when you need it.

Guide to Changing Lines

━⊖━ *on the First Line*

Before you even get started, you're blocked! Step back, define the issues, and identify the resources needed. Meanwhile, call on someone who can see the situation with fresh eyes.

━×━ *on the Second Line*

Be wise: admit when something's not working, consult others, and remain flexible. Remember: you don't have to take advantage of every opportunity that comes along.

━×━ *on the Third Line*

At this time, you lack the expertise to handle this situation correctly. By forging ahead regardless, you're working against your own best interests. Reexamine your goal.

▬×▬ *on the Fourth Line*

Swallow your pride and admit you can't do everything by yourself. Increase your chances of success: buy a guide, hire a consultant, or speak with an expert—quickly!

▬●▬ *on the Fifth Line*

While your goal is clearly defined (perhaps even within view!) you must act with caution, tact, and patience. For now, satisfy yourself with small steps—save the leaps for later.

▬×▬ *on the Sixth Line*

Change is healthy and natural. Resist the resulting opportunities, and you defeat yourself before you begin. Rather than get bogged down in the past, embrace a brighter future.

4

Acting Rashly

The empowered person sees how small springs carve out valleys and become great rivers, and learns lessons about patience, time, and opportunity.

Keywords: Inexperience, enthusiasm, ignorance, imprudent or headstrong action, lacking caution, stubbornness

Encourages: Tempering enthusiasm or energy with restraint; accepting the role of a student; admitting you don't know everything; looking before leaping; controlling impulses; gaining the experience needed to become confident and competent

Cautions against: Being hotheaded; asking the I Ching the same question over and over again; annoying others with improper action or speech; ignoring information which displeases or upsets you; acting like a know-it-all

THOUGHT QUESTIONS

In what ways am I still a beginner? What experience do I lack?

How good am I at controlling rash impulses?

How do I respond when I make a mistake? How should I respond?

How would a total beginner approach my situation?

Commentary

A student who asks the same question over and over does more than annoy the teacher—he also demonstrates his lack of readiness to learn. When you're in a situation that's new to you, it takes modesty and self-discipline to embrace your own ignorance.

Becoming conscious of what you do not know is frequently the first step on the road to growth. Getting all the answers in the world won't help you if you skip the homework that helps you make sense of them. Care for the bubbling spring; the river will follow.

Love & Relationships

Be consistent in what you do; an on-again, off-again approach suggests a lack of commitment. Rather than fill in the blanks, admit what you don't know. Ask questions. To prompt further growth, get back to basics.

Work & Projects

Everyone was once an intern. Lessons learned while you were inexperienced may come in handy now. Embracing your inexperience is most likely the way to make progress. Become more professional by finding an expert and asking good questions.

Guide to Changing Lines

▬x▬ *on the First Line*

Training wheels make sense at first, but eventually, they look ridiculous! Enough scratching the surface! Commit, and gain the knowledge that comes with experience.

▬⊖▬ *on the Second Line*

Meet the shortcomings of others with grace and embrace their inexperience with humility. Maximize your success by recognizing the potential of even the rawest recruit.

▬x▬ *on the Third Line*

Beginners frequently become fanatics (focusing on one thing to the exclusion of others) or dabblers (lacking depth). Avoid both extremes by combining humility, dignity, and patience.

▬x▬ *on the Fourth Line*

Ignorance and foolishness combine to form a self-reinforcing prison. If you refuse to listen to others, you'll become ensnared in a trap of your own making.

━x━ *on the Fifth Line*

Innocent children ask questions without embarrassment. Adopt their approach to life: make inquiries with a sincere heart, and success will be yours.

━⊖━ *on the Sixth Line*

When patient instruction will not do the trick, sometimes punishment is the only option. Control yourself first. When correction is called for, do it gently to avoid rebellion.

Planning Action

As clouds approach, an empowered person prepares for rain.

Keywords: Waiting, preparing, making provision, making ready, training, practicing, pause for reflection

Encourages: Taking advantage of downtime to prepare for future action; waiting until the right time comes along; training and practice; getting things ready for a future event; exercising discipline; getting your bearings

Cautions against: Acting prematurely; ignoring warning signs; failing to prepare for a contingency; wasting time; lacking the discipline to distinguish worktime from playtime; acting without thinking things through

THOUGHT QUESTIONS

How prepared am I? What do I need to do to prepare myself?

What can I do now to make things easier tomorrow?

How successfully am I reading the signs indicating things to come?

What preparations today will make me better positioned for success?

Commentary

The rain will come when it comes. Rather than worry about the rain, we ought to focus on things we can control. Success may be less a matter of watching the skies, and more a matter of building rain barrels.

Waiting is not the same as doing nothing. Take this time to become better informed and more highly skilled. Rather than fret about tomorrow, be in the moment and appreciate what you have today. Face your situation; substitute work for worry.

Love & Relationships

Insecurity never improves your life or your relationship. Instead of worrying about what might happen, pay more attention to what can be done. Where "fools rush in," empowered people watch, wait, and learn. Get some perspective before taking action.

Work & Projects

Certainty is a luxury that business rarely affords. Pause long enough to get your bearings, and use the hiatus to become better prepared to take advantage of opportunities on the horizon. Beware unrealistic thinking. Focus on what you can do right now, today.

Guide to Changing Lines

▬●▬ *on the First Line*

Any problems you anticipate are really pretty far down the road. Instead of investing energy and time in worry, concentrate on maintaining "business as usual."

▬●▬ *on the Second Line*

People may try to provoke you into action with criticism and unwanted advice. Rather than respond, keep your own counsel and move when the time is right.

▬●▬ *on the Third Line*

You've made your situation worse by leaping before looking. All isn't lost, though. You can get out of this mess if you'll focus on taking one step at a time.

▬×▬ *on the Fourth Line*

The knot is tied tightly around you; there's no moving forward or going back, and wiggling makes things worse. Keep a level head, and hold still until things improve.

━●━ *on the Fifth Line*

Things are getting better—but don't drop your guard; this is just the eye of the storm. Take advantage of a resting period, but be ready for the battle to resume soon.

━×━ *on the Sixth Line*

Good news: the waiting is over. Bad news: you're trapped in a pit! Remain alert: help is coming in the form of something or someone completely unexpected. Embrace it.

6

Resolving Conflict

The fact that the sky and sea are permanently divided reminds the empowered person that conflict is inevitable.

Keywords: Conflict, disagreement, clashes, combat, disputes, opposition, differences, struggles, incompatibility, compromise

Encourages: Standing up for what you feel is right; developing common ground; pursuing the trust of others; objectively evaluating your own position; understanding your own motives; keeping a cool head; calling for arbitration; defining how the situation began

Cautions against: Fighting for a cause you don't believe in; moving forward when you know you're in the wrong; believing that might makes right; favoring aggression over agreement; treating the ideas and values of others with disrespect

THOUGHT QUESTIONS

How certain am I that my position is justified? How can I know for sure?

What common ground can I establish with those who oppose me?

What am I willing to give up in a compromise?

What neutral party can help settle this conflict?

Commentary

With the exception of dishonest and immoral persons, most people involved in a conflict believe in the rightness of their position. Rather than force others to see things your way, attune yourself to shared values. To resolve differences, focus on how you're alike.

Conflict disrupts your focus, distracting you from your goal. As a result, moving ahead is not recommended now. If you can't resolve the conflict by focusing on common ground, call in a trusted mediator. Moving ahead regardless will only make things worse.

Love & Relationships

Moving ahead requires understanding as completely as possible the viewpoint of others (and the values which support those viewpoints). In addition, you must also define precisely what you want . . . and the extent to which you're capable of being flexible.

Work & Projects

Though tempted to move ahead regardless, don't undertake new assignments or pursue additional goals until this issue is resolved. The need for a neutral opinion is critical. Keep a cool head. The seeds of this conflict likely hint at its best possible resolution.

Guide to Changing Lines

▬×▬ *on the First Line*

Consider what you may be doing to perpetuate this conflict. While everything will be fine in the long run, prepare in the short term for a minor skirmish.

▬○▬ *on the Second Line*

When you're outgunned and outmaneuvered, engaging in battle invites disaster. Rather than be drawn into unequal conflict, consider the value of a strategic retreat.

▬×▬ *on the Third Line*

Avoid exaggerated claims to fame. Rather than focus on recognition, just do the work. The experience of work is worth far more than the credit others may (or may not) give you.

▬○▬ *on the Fourth Line*

Being able to win a fight doesn't guarantee that your cause is right. Before taking action, objectively evaluate your position . . . and consider alternatives that lead to peace.

━●━ *on the Fifth Line*

If you're on the side of right, you've nothing to fear from the insights of an objective third party. Seek outside counsel, arbitration, or an unbiased opinion—it can't hurt!

━●━ *on the Sixth Line*

Coming out on top doesn't guarantee happiness. What you win today can easily be taken away by others tomorrow. Ask yourself, "Is this battle really worth the effort?"

7

Rallying Others

Valuable water can be hidden underground. The empowered person, knowing this, uses gentle leadership to tap the hidden strengths of everyday people.

Keywords: Gentle leadership, organization, discipline, direction, allegiance, inspiration, patriotism, morale, reward

Encourages: Explaining objectives and goals as a means of inspiring allegiance; earning trust by proving yourself to be a dependable leader; moderating emotions to keep dangerous actions in check

Cautions against: Rallying people around an unjust or unnecessary cause; fanning the flames of fanaticism; engaging in conflict without regard for how everyday people will be impacted

THOUGHT QUESTIONS

How can I most effectively get "buy in" from others?

How can I make sure enthusiasm for this effort doesn't get out of hand?

How can I be sure everyone's energy will be directed in positive, effective ways?

If my real motives are revealed later on, will others be impressed ... or outraged?

Commentary

Any group of people can become a powerful army, given proper leadership and motivation. Good leaders, though, are always mindful of the difference between a disciplined military force and a bloodthirsty rabble.

Unhealthy, unhappy, or misinformed people cannot function at their best. Before you rally the troops (or before you lend your talents to a cause), be sure to identify exactly what must be done, why it must be done, and the concrete benefits of reaching the goal.

Love & Relationships

You can't bring out the best in others by deceiving them. Rather than manipulate those around you, be honest about what you need. Your boldness and clarity will inspire the same qualities in others, tapping a deep, rich well of real happiness in the process.

Work & Projects
In the name of efficiency, it's tempting to plow ahead before getting everyone on board. People want to understand how their contributions influence outcomes! You can boost your chance for success by clarifying the goal and everyone's contribution toward it.

Guide to Changing Lines

━x━ *on the First Line*

Before taking any action, be sure you have a valid, clearly-defined goal—otherwise, you're defeated before you begin.

━❍━ *on the Second Line*

Recognize that the success or failure of your current effort will impact how others evaluate you. What actions can you take to inspire the approval of others?

━x━ *on the Third Line*

Too many cooks spoil the broth! If everyone tries to take the wheel, the car will go off course. Establish order and assign roles, giving each person specific responsibilities.

━x━ *on the Fourth Line*

Persisting in a pointless struggle is a sign of stupidity—not strength. There's a time for orderly retreat. In order to move on, you must first admit what isn't working.

▬x▬ *on the Fifth Line*

When rabbits are gobbling up the garden, fixing the fence can be more effective than butchering bunnies. Identify the real issues . . . and take appropriate action now.

▬x▬ *on the Sixth Line*

Reward should be based on right action—not necessarily on effort. Some work merits advancement . . . but some work merits only recognition. Distinguish between the two!

8

Coming Together

An empowered person notes how rivers flow into the sea, and realizes how small contributions combine to form great forces.

Keywords: Unifying, coming together, joining a group, following a leader, finding your place in an effort, identifying your role

Encourages: Defining the roles of all players; building an appreciation for individual contributions; organizing many around one capable leader; questioning your own fitness for leadership; becoming part of a group; valuing everyone's contribution to an effort

Cautions against: Blindly following inept or dishonest leaders; taking the reins before you are qualified to do so; joining a group too late, after others have forged alliances or built relationships; resisting involvement in the common good

THOUGHT QUESTIONS

How qualified am I to be a leader in this situation?

How might my situation improve if I merged my efforts with like-minded others?

How likely is it that a "latecomer" to this situation can make a contribution?

What do I bring to this situation that no one else does?

Commentary

Just as specific natural laws govern the flow of rivers and streams toward the sea, social and emotional laws govern how people come together. Generally, the efforts of one person unify and motivate others; if you're a good leader, you can do this, too.

With leadership, though, comes responsibility. Examine your worthiness before grabbing the reins! If qualified: by all means, step up to the plate. If not: recognize you still have contributions to make . . . and make them as a follower, not a leader.

Love & Relationships

In a relationship, you don't always have to be in control. Be willing to play a supportive role when situations arise that are better managed by your partner's skill set than your own. Admitting your weaknesses can be as important as exercising your strengths.

Work & Projects

If you've got what it takes to pilot this project, by all means, do so—but not before taking stock of what it is you really have to offer. Leading isn't the only way to excel. Determine how you can best contribute. If that dictates a supporting role, so be it.

Guide to Changing Lines

▬×▬ *on the First Line*

Remain devoted to what you seek, and you will eventually obtain it. Sincerity's the key. While your influence is limited, your dedication enlists aid from those in control.

▬×▬ *on the Second Line*

Look before you leap. Is this call to action worthy of your best work? If so, apply your best efforts and find good company. If not—why waste your time and energy?

▬×▬ *on the Third Line*

Sometimes, we're forced to be close to people out of circumstance, not choice. When this happens, be sociable . . . but reserve intimacy for those who are truly worthy.

▬×▬ *on the Fourth Line*

Once a relationship is well-established with the right person, there's no need to hide it. If you're really prepared to dedicate yourself, let others know which side you're on.

━●━ *on the Fifth Line*

Worthy leaders neither invite followers nor force their compliance. People will be drawn to a deserving person without being compelled to do so. Avoid "buying your friends."

━×━ *on the Sixth Line*

You may have waited too long to take best advantage of this situation. Take stock of the moment, and take action only if you discover you can still participate fully.

9

Taking Small Steps

The empowered person knows light breezes steer mighty clouds.

Keywords: Prioritizing, perspective, immediacy, alertness, subtle influence, baby steps, project management, living in the moment

Encourages: Waiting for a better opportunity; recognizing imperfections in the current opportunity; understanding the larger impact of small actions over time; overcoming large obstacles by taking tiny, deliberate steps; acting with great restraint

Cautions against: Trying to achieve too much too soon; taking rash action before all preparations are made; ignoring small warning signs; attempting to control a situation with a heavy hand; mistaking potential for certainty

THOUGHT QUESTIONS

How certain am I that this is the right time to act?

What little steps can I take today with an eye toward tomorrow's goals?

How can I exercise subtle control over this situation?

What would a restrained or extremely cautious person do right now?

Commentary

Long before a powerful storm arrives, tiny breezes fashion weightless water vapor into monstrous thunderclouds. Storms form only when moisture, pressure, and temperature dictate; wishing for rain before these conditions are met is a waste of time and energy.

Currently, you're surrounded by signs that a goal could be met. These swirl around you, like clouds . . . but trying to force them into formation is pointless. Nudge here; tap there. Be gentle; exercise restraint. Before taking any action, see how the system evolves.

Love & Relationships

The emotional weight of a relationship, taken as a whole, can be overwhelming. Rather than work on "the relationship," focus on the small, moment-to-moment actions that move a relationship along. If these are in order, the relationship takes care of itself.

Work & Projects

How do I get started? When will I get finished? Asking questions like these works against your success. It's better to commit to one small task you can do right now, this minute, and finish it. Approached this way, work seems to complete itself.

Guide to Changing Lines

━⊖━ on the First Line

Action and confrontation aren't the only options here. Rather than force progress, tend to some small matter and avoid making waves. This strategy pays off in the long run.

━⊖━ on the Second Line

Taken at the wrong time, not even the right action will have beneficial effect. Rather than take action for action's sake, pause a moment to learn from the actions of others.

━⊖━ on the Third Line

By pushing forward when waiting would be best, you make things harder (and potentially more embarrassing) for yourself. Obstacles are a message. Are you listening?

━x━ on the Fourth Line

Objective advice—even if painful—benefits you and those around you. If you can't be objective, ask a third party and pay special attention to what you don't want to hear.

━●━ *on the Fifth Line*

People trust a loyal person to honor his commitments and play his assigned role. When everyone involved does this, all benefit. To what extent is this happening now?

━●━ *on the Sixth Line*

Small steps over time are the key to success—but don't drag things out or be too thrilled when you reach your goal. New challenges are close at hand; be ready to start again.

Walking Softly

Lakes and skies never argue over their roles; each knows the value of the other's contribution. The empowered person knows that order and progress hinge on this perspective.

Keywords: Finesse, diplomacy, tact, courtesy, manners, decorum, politeness, political awareness, temper

Encourages: Walking softly while carrying a big stick; keeping your cool while others lose theirs; being polite in difficult situations; calming others with soft responses; identifying common ground as a means of soothing ruffled feathers

Cautions against: Walking over others in an attempt to get what you want; getting caught up in frenzied emotional reactions; returning insult for insult; stirring the pot or contributing to the escalation of hostility; deliberately pushing people's buttons

THOUGHT QUESTIONS

To what extent is my involvement improving this situation?

What do opposing parties have in common? How can this unify them?

How can progress be made in such a way that everyone feels valued?

To what extent do all the players in this situation value the contributions of others?

Commentary

Knowing the value of your own contribution is one thing; recognizing how your contribution combines with those of others is something else entirely. Everyone involved in this situation plays a part in it; understanding and appreciating that fact is critical.

When people adopt a distorted sense of the value of their contribution, chaos reigns. Your success depends on helping everyone involved adjust their perspective . . . without stepping on sensitive toes in the process. Use tact, acknowledge issues, and move on.

Love & Relationships

Failing to do what you can do best. Assuming control over things you don't do well. Both of these are strategies for failure! A relationship depends on each person recognizing the value of the other. Does your partner need to be gently reminded of this? Do you?

Work & Projects

Without belittling or upsetting others, you can improve chances for success by being firm and polite at the same time. That doesn't mean mustering a fake smile while giving orders. Instead, treat everyone (including yourself) humanely while insisting on progress.

Guide to Changing Lines

━●━ *on the First Line*

We cheer for underdogs who rise above adversity with noble purpose, but hate arrogant achievers who forget their humble beginnings. Keep things simple. Progress depends on clarifying and quietly working toward your goals.

━●━ *on the Second Line*

Find the confidence and strength to set your own course. When you do, your fulfillment comes from within, and the opinions and evaluations of others won't matter anymore.

━x━ *on the Third Line*

Everyone has strengths . . . and weaknesses. Moving ahead recklessly exposes your shortcomings and results in a bad situation. Question your motives: are your intentions pure?

➙ on the Fourth Line

Your situation is risky; still, if you'll tread very carefully, you'll succeed. Caution is the key. Since merely "holding the fort" isn't an option, tiptoe mindfully forward.

➙ on the Fifth Line

Stick to your guns. In doing so, you incur risk. Success will still be possible, though, if you're aware of this risk and sensitive to how it impacts those around you.

➙ on the Sixth Line

What's done is done. What outcomes have past actions produced? If you're happy, keep doing what you're doing. If you're not—it's time to change your approach.

11

Working Together

Heaven on earth! The empowered person recognizes the fleeting nature of prosperity and unity, and moves to take best advantage of it, empowering all!

Keywords: Unity, cohesiveness, prosperity, productivity, fairness, respect, mutuality, togetherness, stability

Encourages: Sharing wealth and work; making hay while the sun shines; expecting a change for the better; working to establish heaven on earth; increasing productivity; dividing work fairly among many, and sharing rewards as they come

Cautions against: Hoarding wealth; unequal distribution of work, responsibility, or reward; allowing events to unfold without careful oversight; allowing rampant production to create chaos; expecting prosperity to come about without careful planning

THOUGHT QUESTIONS

What can I do to ensure fairness and mutuality?

What stands between me and productivity?

How is responsibility divided among players in this situation?

How can I contribute to stability and prosperity?

Commentary

Heaven on earth! Is it possible? Yes—when leaders listen to the needs of their people, and the people appreciate and obey their leaders. With everyone and everything in its place, battles end, and a reign of peace begins.

Maintain this period of peace with measured industry. Take advantage of the good energy. Make careful plans. Schedule and complete work you've neglected. More good times are ahead if you'll carefully regulate your awareness and efforts.

Love & Relationships

When two partners honor each other, a relationship is at its best. Don't settle for less. Give your partner his or her due . . . and expect the same in return. That's how things should be . . . and if that's how they are, remember to work to keep them that way.

Work & Projects

Divide and conquer! Break large assignments down into small, approachable pieces. You'll feel less intimidated and more empowered to begin . . . and finish . . . the work. In the meantime, focus on making your best effort. Allow yourself the pleasure of getting lost in good work.

Guide to Changing Lines

▬●▬ *on the First Line*

Times are good, and your influence is more powerful than you know. Draw others to you and get things done while you can. Help others see how they can share in your prosperity.

▬●▬ *on the Second Line*

In times of peace, it's tempting to slack off. Keep two things in mind: deal gently with those who aren't producing, and attend carefully to small details. Seek balance.

▬●▬ *on the Third Line*

Change is constant, and peace will eventually give way to chaos and disruption. Remember: if you establish peace within, you insulate yourself from changes like these.

▬✕▬ *on the Fourth Line*

Rather than boast about your accomplishments or superiority, emphasize what you have in common with others. Focus on your shared humanity, not mere externals.

▬x▬ *on the Fifth Line*

Voluntarily placing yourself in submission to others can be a very effective way to maintain the peace. Be open to a servant's role, and good things will happen.

▬x▬ *on the Sixth Line*

A time of peace begins to pass. Submit to change; resistance will only bring unhappiness and humiliation. Depend on your inner circle, and prepare to weather dramatic change.

12

Falling Apart

In a time when peace declines and good cannot triumph, the empowered person withdraws, reserves strength and influence, and awaits an opportunity to contribute to change.

Keywords: Weakness, harshness, chaos, staleness, stagnation, downward trend, decline, decay, corruption, disintegration, entropy

Encourages: Pausing; taking stock; recognizing a "change in the wind"; acknowledging weaknesses; holding to values in hard times; declining opportunities for ill-gotten profit

Cautions against: Denial that a situation is turning for the worse; taking advantage of others during difficult times; practicing dubious "situational ethics"

THOUGHT QUESTIONS

How realistic am I being about the direction this situation is taking?

How can I avoid lending my influence to harmful projects and undertakings?

How can I remain true to my best path when others abandon theirs?

How can I best prepare myself for a period of "rough weather?"

Commentary

A belief in good fortune requires a belief in ill fortune. The pendulum swings in two directions, and, following a period of especially prosperous times, a cycle of challenges is likely to follow in which good deeds are punished and evil actions are rewarded.

The tide has turned—and will turn again. Rather than be drawn into the general atmosphere of fear, suspicion, mistrust, and ill-intent, withdraw. Don't be tempted or misled by ill-gotten emotional or financial gains. Be true to your own best self.

Love & Relationships

In relationships of any kind, some times are better than others. A rough period begins. Avoid being caught up in anger and drama; instead, pull away just enough to get perspective. Whatever you do, be sure your actions are driven by pure motives.

Work & Projects

For whatever reason, things are disintegrating. Rather than find fault, pull back, take stock of the situation, and embody the highest standards of quality and dedication. Refuse to be involved in pessimism or profiteering. Insulate yourself and weather the storm.

Guide to Changing Lines

━x━ *on the First Line*

During this time of trial, set an example for others. Remain true to your own highest values during this time of trial, and encourage them to do the same.

━x━ *on the Second Line*

Others will flatter you or tempt you to make their decisions for them. Don't be influenced by either activity, even if resistance causes you some suffering. Remain true to yourself.

━x━ *on the Third Line*

While they will not yet admit it, those in the wrong know they've made a mistake. This is a good sign that change is coming, but it is not yet here. Bide your time.

━⊖━ *on the Fourth Line*

Good news: the times are changing. Seizing the lead now could still result in disaster. Success comes to the person who takes control when circumstances offer it.

━⊖━ *on the Fifth Line*

A change in the times, brought on by efforts to restore order, is underway. Enhance your chances of success by authoring a Plan B, C, and D for every Plan A. Be aware and be flexible.

━⊖━ *on the Sixth Line*

A dedication to creativity can put an end to stagnation. Don't sit back and wait. Take a creative, unexpected approach. Put forth an effort, and you'll be rewarded with progress.

13

Getting Along

Flames stretch upward, reaching for heaven. Inspired by this sight, the empowered person reaches even higher by uniting many flames into one bright bonfire.

Keywords: Tolerance, fellowship, allowance, liberality, understanding, acceptance, broad-mindedness, pluralism, confederation

Encourages: Finding unity in diversity; creating an atmosphere of tolerance and mutual support despite differences; forging alliances by valuing the uniqueness of others; providing rules and structure that help people work together; promoting a human agenda

Cautions against: Mixing people and agendas without a plan; trying to organize many different people without the benefit of a strong leader; abandoning plans and being carried along by the flow of events; ignoring the humanity of others; promoting a private agenda

THOUGHT QUESTIONS

How can I appeal to the common values of everyone involved?

What rules are in place that will help everyone get along?

What can be done to appoint a leader everyone will support?

How can I embody the values of tolerance and acceptance today?

Commentary

Flame streams toward the sky, as though desiring a reunion with heaven. Fires burn brighter and higher when many flames are brought together; in your current circumstance, success depends on finding the common ground that unites many into one.

Order and organization are the rule of the day, preferably inspired by a single person with clear vision and the ability to inspire others to set differences aside and work for the common good. To succeed, put personal interests aside, and emphasize the human element in what you're doing.

Love & Relationships

When people come together, they should generate more light and energy than they did when apart. Strengthen your union by focusing on what you have in common. Remember: being strong together depends on having a firm appreciation for yourselves as individuals, too.

Work & Projects

No matter how capable they are, loners can't get as much work done as a dedicated team organized around one inspiring, charismatic leader. You're human; use your human qualities to sense how you can best connect with others to bring about greater success.

Guide to Changing Lines

━●━ *on the First Line*

Avoid any kind of secret arrangement or "back-room dealings." Be open, honest, and above board. Make sure everyone involved shares an equal, informed stake in both risk and success.

━x━ *on the Second Line*

Cliques and side-taking work against your best interest. Resist the urge to paint others in a bad light; ultimately, this is a strategy that will lead to your personal humiliation.

➖ *on the Third Line*

A loss of trust has people guarding their speech and making plans they don't reveal to others. Participating in hidden agendas will only worsen the situation.

➖ *on the Fourth Line*

Things are getting better, and reconciliation is drawing nearer. You still have obstacles to overcome, though. You can get past these more easily if you cooperate instead of compete.

➖ *on the Fifth Line*

Remember: you can be at odds on the outside while still being united at heart. What brought you together in the first place? Emphasize this, and no challenge can drive you apart.

➖ *on the Sixth Line*

Currently, you aren't exactly in sync with people around you, who may also be acting in their own best interests. Seek alliance anyway; together, you can get more done than you can on your own.

14

Having What It Takes

The empowered person knows that, in a dark place, the light from a torch—not the status of the person who carries it—comforts people and draws them together.

Keywords: Courage, ethics, modest leadership, "guts," doing the right thing, grace, clarity, chivalry

Encourages: Standing up for what's right; fighting against what's wrong; surrounding yourself with capable people; being modest about your own capabilities; understanding that even small people may make great contributions; exhibiting grace under pressure

Cautions against: Waiting for someone else to take the reins; being intimidated into silence; blithely enjoying your own blessings while ignoring the perils and trials of others; encouraging a sense of entitlement, greed, or selfishness

THOUGHT QUESTIONS

How can I be sure my motives are the purest they can be?

What small contribution could I make that would have a big impact?

To what extent am I waiting on someone else to "make the first move"?

How can I exercise power in a way that inspires others?

Commentary

A wise man once urged his timid followers not to "hide their candles under baskets." As a leader of men, the wise man understood that, in dark times, even the smallest of lights brings welcome illumination. The presence of the flame matters more than its size.

In this situation, you may feel you lack the status, power, recognition, or knowledge needed to make a real difference. Dispel feelings of inadequacy by realizing that your level of courage and dedication to what's right are the only measurements that matter.

Love & Relationships

In any partnership, one person is very likely more capable, more mature, more attractive, or more successful than the other. Avoid feelings of jealousy and inadequacy by focusing on what small gifts you bring to the relationship. You contribute more than you think.

Work & Projects

You may or may not wear the official title of "leader," but your hard work, dedication to getting things done right, and ability to apply your skills to the challenge at hand can be more inspiring to others (and rewarding to you) than any assigned title.

Guide to Changing Lines

━●━ on the First Line

Rather than be puffed up with pride, keep your own short-comings in mind. Allow others to shine in areas where you're challenged, and transform deficit into opportunity!

━●━ on the Second Line

You'll get more done if you learn to delegate responsibility. Make your talents go further by allowing others to be directed by your insight and influence.

━●━ on the Third Line

A selfish person sings his own praises; a wise person credits others (including higher powers) for his success. Be sure you give credit where credit is due.

━●━ on the Fourth Line

Give up your need to compare your achievements to the achievements of those around you. By focusing on your own efforts, you avoid mistakes.

▬x▬ *on the Fifth Line*

Favor you curry with gifts and bribes won't last long. To build long-term loyalty, you must show a sincere appreciation for the dignity of those around you.

▬●▬ *on the Sixth Line*

Heaven helps those who help themselves. You know the honorable thing to do, so do it. Accept guidance from your higher self, and everything will turn out for the best.

15

Being Modest

Having observed that the sun both rises and sets, the empowered person remains modest—even when enjoying great power and success.

Keywords: Modesty, discretion, balance, equality, prudence, self-effacement, humility, simplicity, lack of pretension, constraint

Encourages: Freedom from vanity; playing down one's own achievements; playing up the achievements of others; doing good in quiet ways; working without worrying about the reward; accepting credit with grace

Cautions against: Being conceited; hogging the limelight; "rubbing in" your success; encouraging or soliciting flattery; possessing an inflated sense of self; having too high an opinion of yourself; putting on airs; false modesty

THOUGHT QUESTIONS

How can I downplay my own contributions and achievements?

How can I accept praise quietly and gracefully?

What can I do to share the limelight with others?

How can I maintain a sense of perspective and balance in this situation?

Commentary

Once the sun rises to its zenith, it has only one option: to come down again. Over time, great mountains become valleys . . . and valleys fill up, becoming plains. The world is in a constant state of flux, raising up what once was lowly and leveling what once was great.

A wise person aligns his or her approach to life with this universal law. When at your lowest, watch for opportunities to build yourself up. When on top, keep your pride in check (and win even more admiration) by practicing restraint and humility.

Love & Relationships

In healthy relationships, what one partner does well often compensates for the other partner's challenges. Look for ways to build up the people around you; in doing so, you'll also motivate them to evaluate your contributions with kindness and affection.

Work & Projects

No one really admires the "glory hog." When others are celebrated, offer your unreserved admiration. When you rise to the top, accept praise with grace and emphasize the contributions of the team. Highlight the success of others as a way of amplifying your own.

Guide to Changing Lines

▬x▬ *on the First Line*

Being modest in your outlook and manner allows you to thrive where others, inflated by their own sense of greatness, would flounder. Keep things simple, and succeed.

▬x▬ *on the Second Line*

While false modesty is never attractive, a sincere expression of your own modesty will earn the respect of others. Remember: what you *say* is often what you are.

▬⊖▬ *on the Third Line*

Get blinded by the spotlight, and you'll lose your way. Keep a level head, though, and you'll find many people will rise to assist you in your pursuit of success.

▬x▬ *on the Fourth Line*

Even modesty can be overdone. Even while being self-effacing, you can be active, engaged, focused, and self-directed. Don't use modesty as an excuse for "slacking off."

━x━ *on the Fifth Line*

The time comes for even a modest person to take prompt, swift action. Don't be a doormat! Respond objectively and firmly. Say what needs to be said.

━x━ *on the Sixth Line*

Refusing to defend yourself or the values you hold dear is not modesty—it's cowardice. To achieve something of value, you must be prepared to stand up for what you believe.

16

Building Enthusiasm

Just as music can unite many bodies in a joyous dance, an empowered person understands what others value and uses this to build unity and spark enthusiasm.

Keywords: Excitement, interest, passion, shared interest, zeal, vigor, zest, gusto, inspiration, eagerness, buzz

Encourages: Uniting individuals by appealing to common interests and values; setting standards that reflect the will of the majority; tapping into whatever truly motivates and delights those around you; aligning your goals with the intent of heaven

Cautions against: Manipulating others; authoring or enforcing laws that run contrary to the will of the people; ignoring the input or responses of others; getting swept up in the thoughtless actions of a mindless crowd; being manipulated by skilled puppeteers

THOUGHT QUESTIONS

How certain am I that my motivations are my own?

What values and goals do the people around me share?

What rewards me? How might the reward preferences of others differ?

What benefits are associated with the solution or action I have in mind?

Commentary

Nature's stable, dependable cycles are governed by the law of least resistance. This principle regulates every conceivable system, from the course of great rivers to the orbits of the planets. You enhance chances for success when you go with the flow.

Rather than force others to adopt your viewpoint, try appealing to common values and goals. Share benefits. Appeal to all the senses. If your motives are pure, there's no harm in wrapping your goals in exciting packages. A little music gets many people dancing.

Love & Relationships

Over time, habits built over months and years can dim the passion you once felt for a partner or friend. Restore a sense of excitement by rediscovering what you have in common right now, today. Your partner's hidden qualities may surprise you.

Work & Projects

Force a product on customers, and you alienate them; offer what they want, and you'll prosper. How many marketing gurus have forgotten this simple concept? Broadcast the honest benefits of your solutions, and others will see the sense and beauty of them.

Guide to Changing Lines

━x━ *on the First Line*

Rather than improve their product, some companies actually hire people to sit in audiences and laugh at bad movies. There's a difference in honest response and forced merriment. Don't pursue or exhibit fake feelings.

━x━ *on the Second Line*

Don't allow enthusiasm to become an anesthetic that numbs your sense of what's going on around you. Enjoy yourself, but monitor the direction of things. Is your destination a healthy one?

━x━ *on the Third Line*

Avoid tying your enthusiasm for something to the behavior of someone else. Depend on yourself to know what's right for you.

━●━ *on the Fourth Line*

Your sincerity is the key to igniting enthusiasm in those around you. Be confident and honest about your goals, and you'll find yourself surrounded by supporters.

━x━ *on the Fifth Line*

You can't be enthusiastic all the time. If you don't feel it, don't fake it.

━x━ *on the Sixth Line*

Tastes change—and wisdom matures over time. What excited you once may not excite you now. Embrace this, and be true to whatever you're feeling in the present time.

17

Adapting to the Times

By sensing and adapting to the change of seasons, an empowered person gains the experience and flexibility that attracts capable followers.

Keywords: Adaptation, adjustment, accommodation, compliance, acclimation, change, evolution, assimilation, conversion, opportunism

Encourages: Adjusting your approach to suit the situation; deferring to others when the situation calls for it; keeping an open mind; placing more value on learning from than on controlling a situation; changing your strategy based on new developments

Cautions against: Doggedly pursuing the same course with no appreciation for how a situation is evolving; committing dogmatically to one solution; refusing to reevaluate earlier decisions; pursuing a one-size-fits-all solution

THOUGHT QUESTIONS

Is it time to pause and reevaluate my response to the situation I'm in?

How can I adapt my plan or approach so that it works better in the here-and-now?

What steps am I taking to monitor the change around me?

How can I best take advantage of the opportunities available now?

Commentary

The only thing that never changes is the fact that things are always changing. What worked yesterday might not work today, and savvy people constantly reinvent their strategies to accommodate new realities as they appear.

What doesn't adapt, dies. Gain wisdom (and the advantage) by evaluating your situation and changing your approach as needed. Rather than bribe weak-minded people or lure others with false promises, allow your insight and adaptability to draw others to you.

Love & Relationships

Relationships grow and change over time. Yesterday's expectations and habits may not apply today. Grow together by talking often about who you are and where you want to be. If single, step outside your comfort zone and reinvent yourself!

Work & Projects

Tried and true strategies worked well in the past, but your environment is changing. Revise your work plan to take changing conditions into account! Schedule constant progress meetings to make sure your approach still makes sense.

Guide to Changing Lines

━⊖━ *on the First Line*

You may be surrounded by "yes men." Before making a final decision, be sure to consult with others who hold drastically different opinions. Unite others by hearing from all.

━×━ *on the Second Line*

If you attach yourself to weak or manipulative people, you won't have room in your life for strong, worthy associates. Evaluate those around you. Are changes needed?

━×━ *on the Third Line*

As you make better and healthier choices, you may have to give up associates and habits that once delighted you. Be true to your own needs, and make changes bravely.

━⊙━ *on the Fourth Line*

If you build yourself up by making selfish choices, the people you attract will be of weak character. Do what you know is right, and earn success with no strings attached.

━⊙━ *on the Fifth Line*

If you are determined to make the best possible choices, you'll succeed. Evaluate your situation, consider what you value most, and make a decisive, fearless choice.

━×━ *on the Sixth Line*

Your evolution and growth hinges upon finding a mentor or guide. Seek someone who's "been there and done that," and learn from his or her example.

18

Correcting Mistakes

The empowered person doesn't just throw out spoiled food; instead, he or she also investigates to discover and correct the condition that caused the spoilage.

Keywords: Repentance, rectification, correction, recovery, reparation, revision, reform, remediation, apology, change of heart

Encourages: Acknowledging mistakes; making amends; admitting imperfections; committing to improvement; taking corrective action; saying "I'm sorry"

Cautions against: Sweeping things under the rug; making things worse by forging ahead regardless; rejecting the possibility of error; justifying wrong action

THOUGHT QUESTIONS

How might I be at fault? How might I make amends for wrong actions?

To what extent has a "change of heart" been followed up by a change in actions?

What steps need to be taken to repair the damage that's been done?

How can you prevent a similar situation from arising in the future?

Commentary

When something goes wrong, don't forget the law of cause and effect. If you continue doing the same things in the same ways, you'll continue to get the same results. Back up. Investigate. Pinpointing the real cause of the problem is the key to solving it.

This situation didn't evolve overnight, and it can't be fixed in a day. You can start, though, by carefully and mindfully investigating what must be changed. When that's done, move ahead cautiously, taking care not to repeat past mistakes.

Love & Relationships

If you're uncomfortable for any reason, you should do more than find out why—you should also develop a plan of action for moving past the discomfort. Analyze the situation, change your approach, and then take action accordingly.

Work & Projects

Simply plowing forward for the sake of progress won't compensate for mistakes made early on. Stop. Back up. Take stock of the situation, and identify exactly where things went wrong. Assign no blame . . . but do learn from mistakes. Then: move forward.

Guide to Changing Lines

━x━ *on the First Line*

Things aren't quite as bad as they seem, but they're compli cated by someone blindly repeating mistakes of the past. Avoid blame . . . and gently stress the benefits of change.

━⊙━ *on the Second Line*

Your situation is rooted in someone's weakness. Forcing drastic change will only deepen old wounds. Suggest small, gentle, baby steps. Consider the feelings of other people.

━⊙━ *on the Third Line*

Some people resent the admission of any mistakes—yours or theirs. Make changes, but prepare for minor flare-ups and ruffled feathers. Persist in what you know is right.

▬x▬ *on the Fourth Line*

You're being tempted to move on without taking steps to correct what's really wrong. Change course now—your current path leads only to humiliation and defeat.

▬x▬ *on the Fifth Line*

Old mistakes complicate your current progress. You can't compensate for these alone. Get others involved in making things right in order to restore forward motion.

▬⊖▬ *on the Sixth Line*

Accept the fact that you alone cannot make amends for certain mistakes. In this case, learn from what you observe, but take no responsibility. Move on, taking care to do no harm.

19

Making Progress

Like the hard-working ant in the children's fable, the empowered person, with an eye on the coming of winter, makes strategic use of warm summer days.

Keywords: Advancement, betterment, improvement, facilitation, opportunity, forward motion, augmentation, increase, acceleration

Encourages: Making hay while the sun shines; blazing new trails; overcoming obstructions; moving on; making the most of a run of good luck; working hard with an eye toward future challenges; answering opportunity's knock

Cautions against: Wasting time; goofing off; embracing stagnation; failing to take advantage of lucky breaks or good offers; failing to follow up on a promising lead;

giving in to distraction or laziness; letting the chips fall where they may

THOUGHT QUESTIONS

How can I get more work done right now . . . today?

What opportunities have I rejected, discounted, or overlooked?

What resources do I need in order to start moving forward again?

How can I let go of the past, so that I can move forward toward my future?

Commentary

You can't do everything yourself . . . but you can make sure you make the most of the time and resources afforded you. Now is a time for work! Check your priorities, set goals, make a list of the small steps needed to achieve your larger goals, and get cracking!

This window of prosperity and good fortune will inevitably give way to a time of challenge and impeded progress—that's the nature of the universe! By working hard now, you can insulate yourself from the impact of unforeseen complications later on.

Love & Relationships

Answer those calls. Go on those dates. Accept invitations. This is the time to make new acquaintances, to strengthen your ties to existing friends and partners, and embrace what life brings your way. Don't let your moods or habits blind you to possibilities!

Work & Projects

This is a good time to overachieve: beat deadlines, work a few extra hours, and, in general, get ahead of yourself. Challenges down the line may impede progress, so take advantage of this opportunity to get ahead of schedule.

Guide to Changing Lines

━❍━ on the First Line

Move forward and make haste, but don't compromise your standards or values while doing so. Progress at any cost isn't progress at all.

━❍━ on the Second Line

If you can manage your own progress, you'll gain valuable maturity. Make a plan and stick to it, and you won't have to worry about the future.

━×━ on the Third Line

When things are going this well, it's tempting to relax and let progress slide. If you've done so, apologize as needed, forgive yourself, pick up the pieces, and move on.

━x━ *on the Fourth Line*

Be open-minded and receptive to advice. Someone you might at first think too inexperienced or powerless to help you has input that will aid you now.

━x━ *on the Fifth Line*

You can't do it all. If you're going to make progress, you're going to have to master the art of delegation. Relax, give up some control, and trust others to work with you.

━x━ *on the Sixth Line*

As you make progress, watch for opportunities to learn from the experience of others—and chances to share your expertise, too. Prepare to get—and give—advice.

20

Inspecting Progress

The empowered person observes how the wind touches every point on earth, and follows this example by going out to see the world with his or her own eyes.

Keywords: Examination, review, evaluation, comparisons, inspections, follow-ups, call-backs, surveillance, supervision, reexamination, overviews

Encourages: Looking in on what's been done; managing by walking around; asking questions; comparing progress to expectations; grading or evaluating output; measuring satisfaction with the situation; taking surveys; assessing growth and fulfillment

Cautions against: Accepting reports or statistics at face value; assuming progress is being made; deluding yourself; practicing selective blindness; insulating yourself from the facts; avoiding criticism or critical thinking; overlooking the need for feedback

THOUGHT QUESTIONS

What's the gap between what I want and what I'm getting?

To what extent have I personally verified what I believe is true?

How happy am I with my progress? With the progress of those around me?

What kind of information or feedback do I tend to reject or overlook?

Commentary

In olden times, rulers often disguised themselves in order to get a firsthand, unfiltered view of the prosperity of their land and the happiness of their people. A good ruler has a specific vision in mind, and inspires others to follow it to the letter.

How long has it been since you surveyed your life and work? It's time to define your expectations and take a frank look at the progress you're making toward living the life you want to live. Be objective, be fearless, and be ruthless. What needs to change?

Love & Relationships

Is the relationship in question (or your personal relationship status) taking you where you want to go? What changes would make you happier? Take action now: express your needs and refuse to settle for anything that doesn't meet your highest standards.

Work & Projects

Who's minding the store? Who's responsible for monitoring overall progress? What are the milestones . . . and what's the status? You need a more holistic vision of what's going on so that you can know with certainty that goals are being met.

Guide to Changing Lines

▬x▬ *on the First Line*

You're not a child anymore! It's time to be more serious about your goals, and more critical of your own progress toward them. Gentle self-discipline goes a long way.

▬x▬ *on the Second Line*

Seeing this situation exclusively from your own viewpoint hinders your progress. To move forward, take time to imagine how all others involved must think and feel.

▬x▬ *on the Third Line*

There's a difference between a self-centered viewpoint and being aware of what you need in order to make personal progress. Define your goal, consider how reaching it will impact others, and then take action.

▬x▬ *on the Fourth Line*

Your position limits your ability to play an active role in shaping circumstances. Rather than give orders, make suggestions or offer advice based on previous experience.

▬⊖▬ *on the Fifth Line*

The only way to know that your efforts are effective is to measure results. What have you done so far? Have you moved closer to your goal in the process? Be objective.

▬⊖▬ *on the Sixth Line*

Set your own concerns aside and look at the situation as objectively as possible. If you were not involved, what outcome would be best? Do what you can, and be at peace.

21

Enforcing the Rules

Upon encountering a stubborn obstacle or a heated disagreement, the empowered person consults the regulations governing the situation and presents a fair-minded solution.

Keywords: Enforcement, conformity, equity, judgment, fairness, trial, jurisdiction, rights, justification, righteousness, legality, appropriateness

Encourages: Calling for mediation; going to a counselor; taking legal action; making an effort to be fair and objective; consulting the rules; accepting the verdict of a judge or referee; dispensing fair and objective justice; making compromises

Cautions against: Mindlessly adhering to arbitrary rules; allowing bias to influence a decision; remaining silent when injustice is being done; stubbornly insisting on a verdict that is solely to your advantage; administering punishment that doesn't fit the crime

THOUGHT QUESTIONS

To what extent am I capable of being fair and unbiased in this situation?

How confident am I that I can resist being swayed by anger or other strong emotions?

What are the rules that govern this situation?

Who could step in to provide a more objective view of this situation?

Commentary

All of us are victims of our own perspective, and none of us is capable of total objectivity. Some, however, are more adept at fairness than others. It's time to move past the drama and get to the root of the real problem.

When someone is in the right, he should triumph. When someone is in the wrong, he should admit it and make amends. To promote fairness and truth, be mindful of the rules, avoid violating them, and insist on justice for yourself and others.

Love & Relationships

When fighting with friends or loved ones, it's easy for emotions to get out of control. What's your real need? What's a fair way to express or fulfill that need? Express what's needed with calmness and directness. Choose to embody fairness and reason.

Work & Projects

Unequal distribution of work, a failure to deal honestly with others, or an unhealthy approach to profit is hindering progress. Shatter the obstacles by reviewing the situation with fairness in mind. Identify the guidelines and make sure everyone follows them.

Guide to Changing Lines

━⊖━ *on the First Line*

Unintentional wrongs or simple mistakes must not be met with fierce discipline or over-the-top punishment. Clear up misunderstandings before things escalate further.

━x━ *on the Second Line*

Who's right? Who's wrong? In this case, it's easy to see . . . but people with agendas or warped values may not share your clear vision. Don't overreact, but stand firm for what's right.

━x━ *on the Third Line*

Someone in a position of power lacks authority, fairness, or worthiness, angering all involved. To move forward, avoid critiquing the judge and focus instead on the fairness of the decision itself.

━❍━ *on the Fourth Line*

The verdict you have in mind is just, but others will strongly oppose it. Stick to your guns. The resistance you'll meet will test the strength of your character and will.

━×━ *on the Fifth Line*

Evaluate the verdict you have in mind by projecting it into the future. What would your conclusion achieve? Will it take you to your preferred destination . . . or closer to danger?

━❍━ *on the Sixth Line*

This situation didn't spring into existence overnight—an observant person would have seen danger signs much earlier. Change your course—or expect great misfortune.

22

Seeing Beyond
the Surface

The empowered person appreciates those qualities which appeal to the eye, but places greater value on those qualities that appeal to the spirit.

Keywords: Appearances, first impressions, hidden depths, character, inner beauty, superficiality, serenity, externals versus internals

Encourages: Believing that beauty is more than skin deep; looking beyond first impressions; pursuing beauty from the inside out; selecting associates with good moral character; caring more about inner qualities than external appearances

Cautions against: making decisions based solely on eye appeal; evaluating people, situations, and opportunities based strictly on outer appearance; attending to cosmetic details when the real problem runs deeper; acting in shallow, superficial ways

THOUGHT QUESTIONS

What's more important: how someone looks, or how someone acts?

To what extent is my judgment being influenced by external factors alone?

How can I free myself from the influence of materialism and consumerism?

Do I pay as much attention to my inner self as I do my outer shell?

Commentary

Beauty and eye-appeal are important, but you mustn't allow them to become the sole basis for the decisions you make. The element that captures your attention most may keep you from seeing other, more important dimensions of your situation.

Be more aware of how you assign value. Avoid being influenced by marketing messages, opinions of others, hearsay, or first impressions. See things more deeply; reflect before you react. You'll grow as a person if your actions are based more on your sense of values than your sense of vision.

Love & Relationships

Life becomes richer when you allow yourself to be attracted by character and compassion. Make sure there's more to your companions (and to you!) than meets the eye. A beautiful spirit persists, even when outer beauty fades.

Work & Projects

When everyone is drawn to high-profile, high-impact work, you can often thrive by paying attention to the small details others ignore. Paying attention to functionality and measurable benefits adds more value than applying a different color paint.

Guide to Changing Lines

━●━ *on the First Line*

Honest intentions are more important than externals now. Move forward by avoiding a "fast and easy" approach and focusing on long-term solutions with greater impact.

━×━ *on the Second Line*

Form . . . or function? If a car has no engine, applying fancy paint jobs and chrome trim wastes time and effort. Attend to core issues before worrying about "looking good."

━●━ *on the Third Line*

There's no harm in appreciating beauty—unless you allow yourself to be so intoxicated by it that you lose all good judgment. Indulge . . . but keep an even keel while doing so.

━x━ *on the Fourth Line*

At some point, even an abundance of comfort can make us feel bewildered and distracted. Simplify, simplify, simplify. Peel back layers and return to what's most important.

━x━ *on the Fifth Line*

You tend to evaluate yourself and your efforts strictly in terms of what you have to offer others. True friends and worthy associates value you for what you are, deep inside.

━●━ *on the Sixth Line*

This situation represents an opportunity to transcend superficiality and show your appreciation for inner value. Focus on function; ignore form.

Tumbling Down

The empowered person evaluates the condition of an old house, and understands the wisdom of moving out before the walls fall in.

Keywords: Breakdown, collapse, dislocation, fatigue, failure, falling, disruption, decay, destruction, dissimilation, degradation, entropy, demolition

Encourages: Clearing ground for new construction; protecting yourself from unfortunate fallout; reading the "signs of the times" and acting accordingly; avoiding action; waiting for a broader base of support before moving forward

Cautions against: Moving forward regardless of ill portents; going down with the ship; remaining in an unhealthy environment for too long; putting all your eggs in one basket; holding to old traditions and approaches after circumstances dictate a new approach

THOUGHT QUESTIONS

To what extent am I being guided by outdated notions of profit or appropriateness?

How willing am I to release the past and be open to new ideas?

What are the signs that it's time to cut my losses and move on?

What needs to be shattered so that I can make progress?

Commentary

There's a time for building up . . . and a time for tearing down. An empowered person understands this, and feels no guilt if he or she needs to retreat in order to await a more opportune moment. Sometimes allowing a collapse is the only way to move ahead.

What needs to be torn down in your life? What could you build if old structures were cleared away? What foundations are beginning to crack? Repair what you can . . . but be willing to admit that some circumstances may not merit your reparative efforts.

Love & Relationships

Wearing yourself out keeping things going? Holding things in so tightly that you almost explode? A relationship shouldn't be this exhausting; something needs to go, so you can relax and grow. If you can't demolish obstacles together, that should tell you something.

Work & Projects
Old habits and old traditions need to be cleared to make way for new growth. If others won't allow for this, don't force it. Instead, do what you can do to make progress and keep careful records so that, when the inevitable happens, you'll be protected.

Guide to Changing Lines

▬x▬ *on the First Line*
Turning this situation around is unlikely; you must decide whether this effort is worth the risk of disaster. It might be good to withdraw now, then wait and see what happens later.

▬x▬ *on the Second Line*
You've been seeing (or ignoring!) signs of a downturn for too long. It's time to change your strategy, get the help you need, and take action to insulate yourself from harm.

▬x▬ *on the Third Line*
Sometimes, disagreements and dissolution open us up to new possibilities. Don't hesitate to get out of a bad situation; often, doing so is the only way to make things better.

━x━ *on the Fourth Line*

Sometimes, all you can do is hang on, take what's coming, and survive it with as much grace as possible. Remember: a broken situation doesn't have to break your spirit.

━x━ *on the Fifth Line*

Take charge of the situation, stressing benefits of your action plan and expressing your opinions bravely. Doing so will unite others and draw their allegiance to you.

━⊖━ *on the Sixth Line*

Take heart: it's always darkest just before dawn. Learn from this misfortune, and allow the mistakes of the past to become seeds for better things in your future.

24

Turning the Corner

The empowered person, observing that the darkness of winter eventually gives way to the brighter days of spring, learns an important life lesson.

Keywords: Rebound, upturn, improvement, advancement, restoration, progress, reform, melioration, betterment, renovation, change for the better

Encourages: Being optimistic; preparing to take advantage of pending improvement; repairing what has been broken; starting fresh; doing spring cleaning; wiping the slate clean; embracing positive change; forgiving and uniting with others

Cautions against: Maintaining pessimism; forcing false happiness or unity before these emotions genuinely occur; persisting with a siege mentality or a victim's mindset; clinging to inappropriate defensive behaviors; resisting renewal

THOUGHT QUESTIONS

What should I be prepared to do as things begin improving?

How should my behavior or thinking change as things get better?

What do I need to do or say in order to start moving forward?

How can I inspire optimism in others?

Commentary

In winter, days get shorter and darkness reaches the height of its power. Eventually, though, the solstice is reached, and slowly, slowly, the light creeps in again. While things have been challenging or difficult for you, take heart: a time of renewal is at hand.

Prepare for beneficial change. Contact old friends. Renew old relationships. Repair personal or professional bridges. Watch for opportunities to agree and work with other people. You've turned the corner . . . so make the most of this time.

Love & Relationships

Relax—things get better from here, particularly if you'll do your part to prepare for growth and improvement. Your situation, having arisen from people avoiding proper action for too long—is ripe for change. Forgive the past and look to the future.

Work & Projects

The worst is over; now it's time to pick up the pieces and move forward. Emphasize tasks and themes that will unite people. Rather than barge ahead, give people (and yourself) time to find natural rhythms again and slowly pick up momentum.

Guide to Changing Lines

━●━ *on the First Line*

Following a rough time, you've stumbled onto the wrong path. Back up and try a new course. Don't fret over your misstep; instead, be determined to make things right.

━×━ *on the Second Line*

Let go of your ego; everyone experiences setbacks, and you're no exception. Make time to talk with people you admire and trust, and commit to doing better in the future.

━×━ *on the Third Line*

The same old habits and a flawed decision-making process threaten to send you back into the abyss! Stop flip-flopping, dedicate yourself to improvement, and move forward.

▬x▬ *on the Fourth Line*

Even when those around you fail to take proper action, you can be inspired by your highest self (or a good role model). Be optimistic even if no one else will be.

▬x▬ *on the Fifth Line*

Instead of making excuses for the errors of the past, admit your mistakes, dedicate yourself to changing your ways, and apologize as needed. No one regrets noble action.

▬x▬ *on the Sixth Line*

Shunning an opportunity to turn things around will bring great misfortune. You are strongly urged to change course and maintain the trend of positive change.

25

Living with Purpose

The empowered person, understanding that a larger plan, often unseen, governs even the most mundane daily events, seeks to live in harmony with that plan.

Keywords: Discipline, focus, intention, innocence, morality, integrity, purity, nobility, holiness, cleanness, mindfulness, balance, flow

Encourages: Aligning yourself with the will of a higher power; making choices with noble goals in mind; meditating and practicing mindfulness; living in a state of grace and innocence; doing your very best; finding and maintaining inner peace

Cautions against: Acting in defiance of nature or God; being guided by selfish or material interests; disregarding instincts and hunches; neglecting the spiritual dimensions of life; taking actions that disrupt harmony and unity

THOUGHT QUESTIONS

In what way might a larger plan be at work in my situation?

How willing am I to trust that some force wants good things for me?

To what extent am I open to being led by intuition, instinct, or "spirit"?

How can I make the healthiest possible choices in this situation?

Commentary

Most people have an innate sense of what would be good and beneficial to do in almost any situation; few, however, have the courage or strength of will to compel themselves to act accordingly. You have an opportunity now to embody blameless innocence. Take it.

You can achieve many things on your own, but what you can achieve when acting in accordance with a larger purpose will astound you. Be open to what your very highest sense of purpose tells you, and you will enjoy great success.

Love & Relationships

Rather than focus on selfish needs, consider actions and strategies that benefit everyone involved in the relationship in question. Deep in your heart, you know what's right here; follow your heart and be open to its message. Be led by love, and do what must be done.

Work & Projects

Give your best effort, even when some slacking might go unnoticed. Resolve to be honest, fair, and above reproach— even if you have only yourself to answer to. Integrity is a rare treasure, but you can possess it. Act accordingly, and enjoy great success.

Guide to Changing Lines

━⊖━ on the First Line

Your heart is a finely tuned instrument. Listen to it. Your first impulses are good ones; go with them, and you'll achieve the best possible outcome.

━x━ on the Second Line

Rather than focus on what was said in the past or what might (or might not) be offered in the future, keep your mind on what you're doing now, and success is yours.

━x━ on the Third Line

Sometimes we suffer setbacks and loss through no fault of our own. Adapt. Make the most of benefits; let go of anything lost. This is the key to balance in your situation.

━●━ *on the Fourth Line*

What really belongs to you can't be stolen. If you reconcile yourself to the idea that no one owns anything but his or her own integrity, no loss can devastate you.

━●━ *on the Fifth Line*

You may be surprised by an attack or other unkind actions launched by others. Rather than fight, be true to your most noble nature. Persist in goodness and move on.

━●━ *on the Sixth Line*

In some situations, no action is the best action. This is one of those times. You can't fix everything, and moving forward now is ill advised. Take a deep breath and wait.

26

Controlling Yourself

To build character, the empowered person makes discipline a habit. When circumstances disrupt his or her habits, the empowered person's strength of character remains.

Keywords: Tenacity, strength, self-discipline, persistence, determination, courage, perseverance, purpose, patience

Encourages: Making and keeping a work schedule; sticking to a diet; exercising self-control, especially in areas that challenge you; practicing beneficial habits; renewing character or spirit through regular meditation; being dependable

Cautions against: Letting yourself go; living without focus or intention; giving into temptations that divert you from your goals; refusing to learn from past mistakes; claiming mastery without putting in adequate practice.

THOUGHT QUESTIONS

What good habits can I adopt in order to strengthen my body and spirit?

To what extent am I in control of my own actions, attitudes, and schedule?

How can I take steps toward establishing a more rhythmic, stable life?

How can I remain focused on my goals despite temptation?

Commentary

Building strength of character takes time. Most people, though, allow whimsy—not practice—to set their standards for self-discipline. They set arbitrary rules or make swift resolutions, then disappoint themselves when they inevitably "fall off the wagon."

Rather than start with rules, begin with goals. What do you want? Where do you want to be? Where are you going? With your vision clearly in mind, discipline is no longer restrictive; instead, restraint becomes a means of attaining what you really desire.

Love & Relationships

Rather than set unrealistic expectations or allow old habits to complicate your relationship, forge new habits, set new goals, and work to achieve them together. Make conscious choices to set personal and mutual directions, and life will be all the richer.

Work & Projects

Haphazard work and progress by "fits and starts" exhausts morale and wastes effort. Define where you are. Define the goal. Analyze the two, listing the specific steps needed to bridge the gap. Divide tasks up into the time remaining ... and stick to the schedule.

Guide to Changing Lines

━●━ *on the First Line*

Action isn't always recommended, called-for, or healthy. Exercise self-restraint in this situation by watching and waiting for the right moment; until then, do nothing.

━●━ *on the Second Line*

Discipline is often a matter of self-restraint. Save your energy; you're going to need it later on. For now, be alert and clear your schedule to prepare for the effort ahead.

━●━ *on the Third Line*

Progress! Obstacles fall away, and forward motion finally occurs. Define your goal clearly and sharpen the skills you'll need to succeed. Get help if you need it.

━x━ *on the Fourth Line*

Channel your energy through discipline. Your art, your work, and your life will benefit greatly. What small steps can you take today toward better self-control?

━x━ *on the Fifth Line*

The force that impels you toward self-destructive behavior, if explored and harnessed, can also propel you toward discipline and success. Take steps now to keep yourself from sabotaging your own best efforts.

━⊙━ *on the Sixth Line*

Obstacles have been cleared away, and the energy you've reserved should now be expressed. Take action now to make your vision a reality, and you'll succeed.

Nurturing Yourself and Others

The empowered person cares for his or her own body and spirit, so that he or she will be better positioned to support and care for others.

Keywords: Guidance, care, encouragement, promotion, advancement, assurance, support, advice, coaching, exhortation, parenting

Encourages: Finding or becoming a mentor; integrating good diet and exercise into your routine and helping others to do so; taking good care of yourself; devoting energy to improving yourself and the world around you, one person at a time

Cautions against: Over- or underindulging in food, drink, sex, or exercise; acting exclusively in your own best interests; refusing the support or guidance of others; believing you can do everything by yourself; acting in self-destructive ways

THOUGHT QUESTIONS

To what extent am I taking good care of myself?

How am I using my talents or skills to improve the lives of others?

What volunteer efforts could benefit from my skills and input?

What is the most nurturing course of action I could take?

Commentary

Your body, and how you treat it, reveals a great deal about the status of your inner growth. Does your body reflect discipline, or license? Does it reflect balance and symmetry, or is it distorted by overemphasis or neglect?

We are both mind and body; both require careful tending and care if we are to be at our best. We cannot adequately care for others until we take good care of ourselves. In this situation, it's time to do what you need to do for you, so you can aid others, too.

Love & Relationships

What percentage of your mutual time is spent nurturing and caring for each other? Consider this carefully, as problematic relationships have often drifted into a pattern of mere coexistence or habitual association. How can you care for your partner's needs?

Work & Projects

Sometimes, the greater good is served by doing what you need to do for yourself first. You may also produce better work by focusing on benefits: how this project will benefit you first . . . and improve the lives of others, later. (If this isn't the case, why invest yourself in this effort?)

Guide to Changing Lines

▬⊖▬ *on the First Line*

Rather than envy the empowered states of others, you should focus on empowering yourself. Let discontent spur action, not contempt and despair.

▬×▬ *on the Second Line*

It's unhealthy to always be the person receiving nurturing from others. Avoid misfortune in this circumstance by finding a way to fulfill your duty to care for others, too.

▬×▬ *on the Third Line*

What you want is not always a good guide to what you really need—ask an addict. Break the cycle of addictive behavior now by clarifying healthy choices and letting go of unprofitable distractions.

▬x▬ *on the Fourth Line*

You've got great intentions, and your zeal enables you to envision more than you can do alone. Amplify your effort by enlisting others to assist you.

▬x▬ *on the Fifth Line*

You're aware of the need for change, but you lack the strength to achieve that change on your own. Call for help. By admitting your need for aid, you're helping others, too.

▬o▬ *on the Sixth Line*

Your ability to guide and nurture others has the potential to create enormous good and generate great progress. Be confident and proceed—but don't forget to also take care of yourself!

Shifting the Burden

The empowered person senses when limits have been reached, and takes action to prevent breakage and collapse.

Keywords: Relief, support, respite, rest, assistance, re-arrangement, reassignment, filling in, moderation, re-prieve, solace, charity, alleviation

Encourages: Redistributing work or responsibility; assessing or anticipating issues and curtailing them in advance; sensing the "breaking point" and taking care not to cross it; asking for help with a difficult burden or complex situation

Cautions against: Taking everything on yourself; unnecessarily playing the role of the martyr; refusing to pay attention to danger signs; "blowing off" indicators that something is going wrong; forgoing opportunities to help others with their burdens.

THOUGHT QUESTIONS

How aware are you of your own limits? What can you do
to honor them?

When is enough . . . really enough?

How can work or responsibility be reassigned or redis-
tributed?

How can I make the most of my strengths, while shoring
up my challenges?

Commentary

The time to repair a dam is when the first tiny crack appears; wouldn't you rather deal with a leak than a flood?
In your situation, pressure is building and building and
building. Doing nothing now is a sure formula for disaster later on.

Get help. Ask someone else to bear part of the load, or
encourage others to redistribute their work so more people
are involved in reaching the goal. Use gentle persuasion
(not force!) to nip the potential for trouble in the bud.

Love & Relationships

Someone is going to burst if this situation continues. You've
acknowledged that there's a problem . . . so now it's time to
commit to an exploration of what's needed to relieve the
pressure. Gently reveal what you've observed, and move
forward with sensitivity.

Work & Projects

It's time for a realistic assessment of your situation. Things can't go on as they are now, so it's probably up to you to suggest changes in a language that enlists the aid of others. Revise deadlines, adjust work schedules, edit task lists . . . before you reach the point of no return.

Guide to Changing Lines

━x━ *on the First Line*

Exceptional times call for exceptional actions. Move forward, but do so very gingerly. Go out of your way to be cautious while building a foundation for moving ahead.

━⊖━ *on the Second Line*

Unusual circumstances call for unusual strategies. What rules, if broken, would immediately improve your situation? What assumptions can you defy?

━⊖━ *on the Third Line*

You can't fix this situation by plowing blithely ahead while everything collapses around you. Change course, reevaluate your strategy, and get help . . . or suffer the consequences.

━⊖━ *on the Fourth Line*

Help comes from unexpected quarters—perhaps by drawing on a resource or idea that's been previously discarded or judged inadequate. Do what's best for the group, not just yourself.

━⊖━ *on the Fifth Line*

A solution isn't worthy or effective just because it's strange or unexpected. Rather than pour energy into something risky or bizarre, why not seek a more moderate path?

━x━ *on the Sixth Line*

Sometimes, extreme personal sacrifice is called for. It may not prevent misfortune, but at least you'll have done everything you can. Forge ahead and do your best, regardless.

Responding to Challenges

The empowered person observes how water changes its shape to fill any space it encounters, and learns a lesson about survival, success, flexibility, and consistency.

Keywords: Resourcefulness, responsiveness, appropriate action, mutability, flexibility, gumption, innovation, invention

Encourages: Responding to crisis with thoughtful action; reading the signs of the times; going with the flow; quickly adapting to new circumstances; reinventing yourself or your strategy to deal more effectively with your situation

Cautions against: Reacting without thinking; resisting change; forcing adherence to a strategy that is no longer appropriate; clinging to old or traditional approaches that have outlived their usefulness; digging in your heels for no good reason; being stubborn

THOUGHT QUESTIONS

How have my circumstances changed? How should I change in response?

What old habits or reactions may keep me from making the best of this situation?

How might an obstacle, challenge, or emergency ultimately prove beneficial for me?

How can I respond to the changing situation without losing sight of my goal?

Commentary

Walking our own best path doesn't allow us to bypass all difficulty; instead, as people in search of our own best path, we resolve to meet difficulties with creativity and faith. We are not the events that surround us; if we control ourselves, our essential character never changes.

The current circumstance demands flexibility, but a change of strategy shouldn't disrupt your vision or force you to abandon your ethics and character. A test like this one prepares you to be consistent in times of much greater trial. Remain focused; move on.

Love & Relationships

Every relationship has its challenges, so be flexible. However, any relationship that demands you sacrifice your dreams, your ethics, or your essential nature should be regarded as suspect. Adapt, but don't give up your personhood in the process.

Work & Projects

Strategies shift, deadlines drift, and what seemed set in stone yesterday is being questioned today. Rather than be overwhelmed, go with the flow. Today brings a new reality; adapt, go where the energy takes you, and success is assured.

Guide to Changing Lines

━✕━ *on the First Line*

Careful: while you should be flexible, you aren't meant to survive in a constant state of flux and disruption. To preserve health and sanity, set some ground rules and limits.

━━ *on the Second Line*

Rather than jump at the first solution that comes your way, face obstacles with mindfulness and critical thought. Weigh options. Small steps may work best now.

▬x▬ *on the Third Line*

In this situation, any action you take will only degrade things further. Rather than force movement now, wait. When the best escape route presents itself, you'll know it.

▬x▬ *on the Fourth Line*

A time comes for questioning rules and breaking with protocol. Extreme conditions call for extreme measures. Try putting people or objects to unusual uses.

▬o▬ *on the Fifth Line*

Now isn't the time for highly successful efforts. Rather than try to excel, simply go with the flow. With time, you'll move past resistance and be successful again.

▬x▬ *on the Sixth Line*

You're encountering obstacles because you're off your own best path. Want things to improve? Invest time in regaining your original vision and direction.

30

Setting an Example

The empowered person, realizing that his or her actions set the standard for others to follow, always seeks to be a light for those who are trapped in darkness.

Keywords: Example, model, role model, template, pattern, illustration, object lesson, illustration, exemplary action, leadership, precedent

Encourages: Doing your best regardless of the circumstances; understanding your own role as a role model for others; considering how an action or statement will impact other people; acting, thinking, or speaking in ways that exemplify how you want to act, think, or speak

Cautions against: Expecting others to do as you say, not do as you do; being a hypocrite; ignoring the good example of others; aligning yourself with someone who sets a bad example; choosing the wrong mentor or hero

THOUGHT QUESTIONS

What would be the impact if everyone acted as I am acting now?

How aware am I of the fact that others are looking to me for guidance?

If I were at my very best, how would I behave in this situation?

What would a worthy hero do in this situation?

Commentary

Every action is an opportunity to set an example. How we treat ourselves, others, and the world around us becomes a template that someone, somewhere, will copy. People are watching; what are you teaching them?

Attend first to your inner character; if it is mature and disciplined, then your actions will be suitable, regardless of the consequence. Like it or not, your light is shining. How can you make sure, in this case, that what you do will be a worthy example?

Love & Relationships

How you treat yourself and how you treat others sets the standard others will use when deciding how to treat you.

Are you fair-minded, patient, and calm? If so, you increase the chances others will be, as well. Let your behavior set a standard for others to meet.

Work & Projects

What if everyone around you put in exactly as much effort as you do? Would work be finished more quickly? Would it take longer? Would it grind to a halt? Your actions telegraph expectations; be careful what standards you're setting for others.

Guide to Changing Lines

━●━ *on the First Line*

Start frazzled, end frazzled. Limit distraction and the potential for drift by starting things off with a clear statement of vision: where you want to go, and how you'll get there.

━x━ *on the Second Line*

The time is favorable for great success. Allow your thoughts and deeds to embody the highest standards, and the brilliant light of your example will encourage others, too.

━●━ *on the Third Line*

Times of transition and challenge often drive people to extremes of pessimism or optimism. Avoid the extremes: exemplify balance by waiting to see what comes your way.

━━●━ *on the Fourth Line*

Sudden action consumes resources and depletes morale. Rather than give in to flare-ups, plan carefully so you can exemplify the power of slow, deliberate progress.

━x━ *on the Fifth Line*

What you are feeling and experiencing now are not expressions of emotional turmoil, but signs that your perspective is changing. Get clarity. Knowing what you really think will help you set your best possible course.

━━●━ *on the Sixth Line*

Rather than use harsh restrictions to control direction, expect individual leaders (beginning with yourself) to set the standard others must follow.

31

Taking Direction

The empowered person remains humble and receptive, encourages others to provide direction and advice, weighs that advice in his or her heart, and takes appropriate action.

Keywords: Influence, inspiration, advice, persuasion, pull, charm, clout, prompt, pressure, inclination, manipulation, enticement, gravitation

Encourages: Being receptive; allowing others to take the lead; being open to other ideas and perspectives; responding appropriately to well-intended guidance; following a good example; valuing the advice offered by respected friends and family

Cautions against: Being manipulated by the agendas of others; being swayed by the opinions of others because you have no opinions of your own; squelching your own preferences to "keep the peace"; giving in to peer pressure

THOUGHT QUESTIONS

How open am I to good advice?

What standard should I use when evaluating advice from others?

What kinds of appeal tend to influence me the most?

To what extent might someone be manipulating me in this situation?

Commentary

Strive to be considered someone who *receives* advice well. Note the emphasis on the word "receives"! Receiving advice doesn't require you to take it . . . receiving requires humility, patience, the ability to listen, and gratitude— nothing more.

If you gain a reputation as someone incapable of tolerating advice, those with anything of value to offer will eventually avoid you. Be open to guidance, and you will soon be surrounded by wise guides you can call on in a circumstance like this one.

Love & Relationships

If you trust the other person in this relationship, it may be time to take seriously what he or she is telling you through words and actions. If you don't trust the other person, or suspect ill intent, you should be wary of manipulation, and proceed with caution.

Work & Projects

Listening to input from others—including subordinates—doesn't require you to give up an ounce of authority. (In fact, being open to suggestions may well cause others to regard you as a stronger leader!) What can be done to encourage openness and good feedback?

Guide to Changing Lines

━x━ *on the First Line*

Until an influence leads to action, it holds no real power. Listen, take recommendations, and seek advice . . . but take no action until you're sure of your own best path.

━x━ *on the Second Line*

The opinions of others hold too much sway over you. Take no action at all until you have formed your own opinions and can say with clarity, "This is what I want."

━◆━ *on the Third Line*

Don't try so hard to influence or solicit the opinions of others. Instead, focus for now on self-discipline, even if that means refraining from doing something you really want to do.

━⊖━ *on the Fourth Line*

The impulses you feel now come straight from the heart. Take appropriate action—but also be sure that as you influence others, you don't give in to the urge to manipulate them.

━⊖━ *on the Fifth Line*

Begin by identifying what you really hope to achieve. While being open to advice, don't allow anyone to sway you from your ultimate goal.

━x━ *on the Sixth Line*

Don't allow yourself to be influenced by empty promises or senseless chatter. If words have nothing of value behind them, they can and should be disregarded.

Maintaining Progress

The empowered person observes the fluctuating cycles in nature, and concludes that maintaining progress requires identifying and working with the rhythms of life.

Keywords: Endurance, unity, stamina, survival, hardiness, continuation, perpetuation, prolongation, protraction, persistence

Encourages: Becoming aware of the cycles of "ups and downs" in your life and work; planning ahead; saving in times of plenty and living frugally in times of famine; embracing the cyclical nature of life; moving ahead while adapting to change

Cautions against: Believing that conditions will always remain favorable or unfavorable; refusing to plan for the future; living strictly for today; pining for the "good old days"; limiting plans to the short-term only

THOUGHT QUESTIONS

How does my situation change over time? Are any cycles apparent?

What natural cycles (moon phases, the passage of years) influence this situation?

How can I anticipate and plan for change?

To what extent have I defined a series of contingency plans?

Commentary

The moon waxes and wanes. Tides rise and fall. Seasons come and go. We live and work in a sea of constant fluctuation—a reminder that all things change over time. Embracing this truth means our plans for the future must take such changes into account.

Maintaining progress requires us to plan for change—otherwise, the smallest alteration in our environment brings progress to a halt. Awareness is the key. How familiar are you with your situation's history? How might the past be useful when predicting the future?

Love & Relationships

Over time, passion and attraction—romantic or otherwise—also wax and wane. An awareness of your own rhythms helps average out the extremes and prevents you from mistaking a temporary "rough patch" for genuine decay. For now, watch and wait.

Work & Projects

In order to bring some objectivity to a highly charged situation, map the course of events over time. What trends can you establish? Maintain progress by reading the situation as accurately as possible, insulating yourself from shrill or overly optimistic influences.

Guide to Changing Lines

▬✕▬ *on the First Line*

Real progress requires consistent work toward a specific goal for a long period of time. Be wary of going too far, too soon—a strategy producing change, but rarely progress.

▬⊖▬ *on the Second Line*

You can do more than you think you can. Take advantage of the enormous potential for progress in this moment, test your limits, and surprise yourself with what's possible.

▬⊖▬ *on the Third Line*

Whimsical and unpredictable moods govern your situation. Step back, take a deep breath, and restore a sense of order and calmness. Don't move ahead until you do.

▬⊝▬ *on the Fourth Line*

How can you expect a different outcome when you keep doing the same thing in the same way? Change your approach. Fresh answers await you in unexpected places.

▬×▬ *on the Fifth Line*

New situations may require you to reinterpret your role or rethink your approach. Maintain your ethics and strength of character . . . but don't hesitate to part with tradition.

▬×▬ *on the Sixth Line*

Progress! Progress! Progress! An obsessive emphasis on moving forward at any cost exhausts everyone. Stop. Catch your breath. Identify the real goal before moving on.

Stepping Back

The empowered person, having recognized the approach of an unfavorable season, reserves his or her strength for a more favorable time.

Keywords: Retreat, withdrawal, backing out, retirement, seclusion, relinquishment, retraction, change of course, reclusiveness

Encourages: Orchestrating a strategic withdrawal; acknowledging the approach of problematic circumstances; seeking seclusion; implementing opposition through subtle resistance instead of outright attack; meditating and reflecting instead of acting

Cautions against: Giving up without a plan for recovery; abandoning an effort or relationship without having plans for the future; blindly fleeing a bad situation; being so caught up in the moment you act without thinking

THOUGHT QUESTIONS

How can I limit my involvement without totally withdrawing?

How can I achieve some perspective? How can I get some emotional distance?

What danger signs are evident? How can I protect myself?

At what point am I prepared to walk away from a bad situation?

Commentary

When darkness falls, the light retreats . . . so that it can return again, revitalized, restored, and renewed. Some circumstances call for a tactical, mindful retreat—not a blind, willy-nilly "running away," but a calculated withdrawal paired with a plan for future action.

This can be done in many ways. A personal retreat is a good idea—a time for contemplating goals and restoring perspective. You can also resist something without opposing it outright; more subtle options often work as well as an outright withdrawal.

Love & Relationships

Your heart already senses the direction of events; it's up to you, now, to take the most appropriate action. Some downtime will restore perspective and create new options. Meanwhile, take measures to insulate your heart from the rough weather to come.

Work & Projects

Moving ahead, given the direction of events, will be extremely difficult. Abandon a project or job only if doing so without risking your well-being and livelihood. The goal, remember, is to improve your situation, not make it more desperate. Don't react; respond instead.

Guide to Changing Lines

━✕━ *on the First Line*

The situation is worsening, and most any action you take now could contribute to making things worse. Consider the wisdom of, for the moment, just standing still.

━✕━ *on the Second Line*

The situation isn't favorable just now, and you may be tempted to throw in the towel. If you're certain your course of action is justified, persist, even when others oppose you.

━○━ *on the Third Line*

A clean break is difficult now, as others, influenced by your decisions, are clinging to you. Take heed of them, but don't allow their concerns to govern your actions.

━●━ *on the Fourth Line*

Work to achieve a friendly withdrawal; part on good terms. Burning bridges as you go will only cause misfortune in the future.

━●━ *on the Fifth Line*

Schedule your withdrawal from this situation, observing all the forms required by friendliness and respect. Others will try to sway you; remain true to your goals.

━●━ *on the Sixth Line*

You've achieved an emotional and personal distance; when the time comes, you can depart with confidence. A cheerful mood helps indicate the "ripeness" of the time.

34

Restraining Impulsiveness

The empowered person makes meaningful progress by taking right action, fueled by right intentions, at just the right time.

Keywords: Self-examination, soul-searching, rationality, psychology, analysis, guidance, conscience, awareness of bias, assumption, motivation

Encourages: Waiting until the time is right; freeing yourself from the grip and pressure of unruly desire; consciously analyzing your own motives; gaining the maturity and strength of character needed to channel energy in positive, calculated directions

Cautions against: Plunging ahead out of enthusiasm or immaturity; chasing a goal willy-nilly; taking action just because you can, without regard for that action's impact on the future; making rash decisions; being inflamed by hype that shuts down rationality

THOUGHT QUESTIONS

How certain am I that the time is right for the action I'm considering?

To what extent is my desire to act motivated by rational thought?

What would happen if I waited a day? A week? A month? A year?

How can I get a clear handle on my own motivations in this situation?

Commentary

Excitement and desire unite, pressuring you to take action immediately. Just because you *can* take action, however, doesn't mean you *should* take action. Reason and action should go hand in hand, so make sure rationality and awareness inform this opportunity.

Capability exercised without reason is just blind force. Insulate yourself from the allure of the merely possible by focusing on slow, steady progress toward larger goals. Remember: there are no shortcuts to real progress, so act with maturity and restraint.

Love & Relationships

Begin with an examination of your goals and motives. What do you really want? Why do you want it? Is what you want really best for everyone involved? Avoid any action born of pressure. Instead, seek a solution that takes you closer to where you want to be.

Work & Projects

Especially in the professional arena, we're often pressured to "strike while the iron is hot." What should govern your progress: the temperature of a hunk of metal, or your own personal direction and goals? Depend on your strength of character to be your best guide.

Guide to Changing Lines

━●━ *on the First Line*

Time to check your motivations. There's a good chance emphasis has been misplaced, and that you're putting too much value on unimportant things. Change course now.

━●━ *on the Second Line*

You're so close, you can smell the success! This proximity to achievement may tempt you to act before the time is right. Keep moving forward, but don't lunge toward the goal.

━⊖━ *on the Third Line*

Some people make progress just so they can boast about it. Avoid this disempowering trap by reserving your ability to act until you're confident that action is the best option.

━⊖━ *on the Fourth Line*

You're facing obstacles, but persistent, small forward motion over a long period of time will move you "magically" past them. With consistent effort, you'll move mountains.

━x━ *on the Fifth Line*

Obstacles fall away easily, so there's no need for an attention-getting show of force. Move forward with confidence and you'll meet little, if any, resistance.

━x━ *on the Sixth Line*

A dead end may complicate progress. Rather than flail around, consider the wisdom of admitting the insurmountable. Retreat, regroup, and try another approach.

Seizing the Moment

When the empowered person sees the sunrise, it dawns on him or her that the proper time for confident action has come.

Keywords: *Carpe diem*, advancement, forward motion, progress, movement, fortuitous or auspicious time, favorable conditions, serendipity

Encourages: Launching a plan; making the most of an opportunity; putting events into motion; acting in accordance with your own best nature; pursuing a reward; rallying the troops; attaining the clarity needed to act with total confidence

Cautions against: Plowing ahead in a bullheaded way; acting purely out of raw self-interest without regard for others; leading where others are unwilling to follow; forcing forward motion at an inopportune time; acting out of reflex or habit

THOUGHT QUESTIONS

What are the signs that this is, indeed, the best moment for action?

What action would I take if I knew this moment was the most fortuitous of all?

How can I move forward in a way that excites and energizes others?

To what extent is my urge to make progress rooted in observation and careful timing?

Commentary

After a long, dark night, dawn breaks. Just as the morning light highlights details in the surrounding countryside, this moment lends clarity to our situation. If we've used our downtime to plan for the future, the sunrise becomes a call to action.

Even under these conditions, with progress so easy and rewards close at hand, you must make sure your actions are guided by selflessness and a sincere desire to make good things happen for everyone involved. If that's the case—go! Success is assured.

Love & Relationships

True love—whether for spouses, partners, friends, or neighbors—puts others before self. This time is especially favorable for mutual progress; watch for opportunities to take an action that benefits you both. Are your motives pure? If so, expect great progress.

Work & Projects

A worthy effort leaps ahead almost effortlessly. Use this energy and "make hay while the sun shines." Encouraging everyone involved to shine and allowing your peers to share in the reward to come increases your status and magnifies your success.

Guide to Changing Lines

▬x▬ *on the First Line*

Others who lack your perspective may insist now is not the time for progress. Without being forceful, use your positive energy and charisma to turn the situation around.

▬x▬ *on the Second Line*

Before seizing this moment, make sure all your ducks are in a row. Is everyone on board? Are higher-ups in tune with your ideas? Confirm commitment before leaping forward.

▬x▬ *on the Third Line*

Your attempts to move forward will enjoy greater success if they are supported by like-minded others. Don't let pride keep you from asking for much-needed assistance.

━○━ *on the Fourth Line*

In this fortuitous time, even someone selfish, undeserving, and weak can easily move forward. Take care; time will eventually deal woe to those with impure motives.

━×━ *on the Fifth Line*

Still feeling cautious, despite assurance that now is the time to act? Don't be hard on yourself. Instead, respect what your heart tells you, and things will work out.

━○━ *on the Sixth Line*

As you progress, deal frankly and fairly with mistakes made by yourself or others, but be forgiving and patient with those whose actions are beyond your control.

Surviving Dark Times

The empowered person, upon encountering a time of darkness, acquires and offers protection, limits movement, and awaits an opportunity to restore the light.

Keywords: Adversity, difficulty, misfortune, distress, disaster, low point, trouble, catastrophe, struggle, affliction

Encourages: Handling adversity with courage; maintaining an optimistic outlook despite dark omens; understanding that times of disruption often create new opportunities; facing difficulty with courage; enduring trials by focusing on the ultimate goal; helping others

Cautions against: Partaking in darkness in an effort to prosper from it; profiteering; falling under the spell of a negative influence; being swayed by friends or companions of questionable character; being swept up in riots, negative thinking, or evil-doing

THOUGHT QUESTIONS

How can I best care for myself and those I love during this time?

What opportunities may arise out of this disorder and disruption?

How can I insulate myself from negativity and inappropriate intent?

How can I recognize the opportunity to take positive action when it comes?

Commentary

Cycles of light and dark are an inherent part of nature. Progress and productivity are inevitable . . . and so are challenges and adversity. Rather than be destroyed by the eventual arrival of darkness, we should prepare ourselves to handle this time with grace.

External circumstances do not dictate your outlook or your character. Remain strong. In order to take advantage of a coming turnaround, you may have to lie low today. Be reserved. Don't reveal or share everything you know. Be cautious and reserved.

Love & Relationships

Resist the urge to compromise your standards and goals. Step out of the spotlight, though, and avoid calling unnecessary attention to yourself. Don't say everything you think, don't believe everything you hear, and, above all, resist the pull of harshness and negativity.

Work & Projects

Active resistance or open rebellion is not an option at this time. This is not a time to call attention to yourself, so play it cool, keep your cards close to the vest, and stay calm. Avoid being caught up in squabbles, blame, and treachery. Rise above the fray.

Guide to Changing Lines

━●━ *on the First Line*

Sticking to your principles in this situation may cost you the affection or respect of those with weaker character. Remain true to yourself, despite temporary social consequences.

━×━ *on the Second Line*

The situation is challenging for you, but potentially devastating for those around you. Your best course of action includes assuring that significant others are cared for.

━●━ *on the Third Line*

The conditions creating this challenge have been in play for a long time, so they won't vanish overnight. Still, a lucky break will present an opportunity for unexpected progress.

▬x▬ *on the Fourth Line*

Coming soon: sudden insights into the real source of your misfortune. Perform a level-headed assessment of the situation, be realistic, and take action to protect yourself.

▬x▬ *on the Fifth Line*

If you cannot withdraw from the situation, then you must insulate yourself from it as much as possible. Success depends on the exercise of extreme caution.

▬x▬ *on the Sixth Line*

Darkness breeds darkness, so evil, at first, appears to grow stronger. Eventually, however, evil collapses under its own weight. Rapid change and swift improvement are at hand.

Establishing Order

The empowered person clarifies expectations and supports the rule of law, knowing that structure and order, when founded on fairness, foster progress and productivity.

Keywords: Role, contribution, rank, structure, chain of command, procedure, rules, hierarchy, management, arrangement, delegation

Encourages: Finding your place in a larger order; working your personal contribution into a larger plan; clarifying expectations; answering questions; authoring and upholding fair laws; respecting and obeying right-minded authority; fulfilling your assigned role

Cautions against: Disrupting order; refusing to fulfill the duties of your position; agreeing to then failing to fulfill obligations; assuming or demanding authority to which you have no valid claim; "lording it over" others; feeling you are "above the law"

THOUGHT QUESTIONS

What is expected of someone in my position? What would be forbidden?

To what extent am I fulfilling my obligations?

What are the rules that govern this situation? Who enforces them?

To what extent have expectations been set and the rules clarified?

Commentary

In a functional family, each person acts with confidence. Expectations, limits, and obligations are clearly defined. Those with authority exercise power with compassion, and others, led by trust and respect, willingly submit to the household order.

To maintain this delicate balance of power, we must possess the wisdom to lead—and be led—as circumstances dictate. Consistency and fairness are critical, and each person must recognize how his actions impact or inspire the others.

Love & Relationships

What rules govern your relationship? What roles have been defined? What obligations created? Unless you know this, you cannot evaluate anyone's contribution. Clarify roles, and bear in mind that, in relationships, respect is earned, but authority exists strictly by mutual agreement.

Work & Projects

Who's in charge? Smooth operation requires capable leadership and appropriate delegation of duty. If problems occur, revisit how time and resources have been divided. You may discover an inequity that limits your potential for success.

Guide to Changing Lines

━●━ *on the First Line*

Clarifying expectations early may ruffle some feathers, but it avoids confusion and remorse later on. Outline duties and responsibilities now.

━x━ *on the Second Line*

The same person can't always set the pace or be the leader. Accept the responsibility that has fallen to you in this matter, and fulfill your duty with all your might.

━●━ *on the Third Line*

A tendency to micromanage things must be kept in check. Define larger roles and general goals, and allow others the freedom to operate within those guidelines.

▬×▬ *on the Fourth Line*

Careful accounting of the situation is called for. To what extent have obligations been met? To what extent have duties been fulfilled? Rely on objective information for answers.

▬○▬ *on the Fifth Line*

Rather than enforce leadership with fear or titles, guide others in love. Stress benefits. Be sincere. Trust evolves when we treat others fairly over long periods of time.

▬○▬ *on the Sixth Line*

If your effort commands respect and stands up to close examination, you'll be respected, and the outcome will be very good. Remember: every leader sets a tone. What's yours?

38

Resolving Tensions

Rather than allow fire and water to extinguish each other, the empowered person combines the two to produce valuable hot water and powerful steam.

Keywords: Conflict, opposition, opponents, obstacles, blockage, reversals, negativity, antagonism, contradictions, rebellion, competition

Encourages: Looking for common ground; exploring mutually beneficial options; overcoming resistance by focusing on the benefits of progress; achieving integration of opposites through slow, deliberate, and careful experimentation; negotiating solutions

Cautions against: Resolving differences through force; attempting to smash through blockages without understanding their underlying cause; open expressions of negativity or antagonism; resisting progress for the sake of resistance alone

THOUGHT QUESTIONS

What do I have in common with those who oppose me?

What will I earn or achieve if I manage to break through this resistance?

How might structure—a schedule, or a set of rules—aid in resolving resistance?

How might two extreme views be fused into one, more moderate opinion?

Commentary

Resistance is any force—internal or external—that works against us. The key to moving past it? Remaining focused on our eventual goal. Small steps, taken daily, yield great progress. Small statements, offered gently over time, change minds and hearts.

Rather than get caught up in name-calling, "he said, she said," or extreme and dogmatic points of view, try finding the middle ground. The universe isn't binary, after all, and truth is frequently found within the shades of gray. What can be blended together?

Love & Relationships

Begin by trying to see and understand viewpoints other than your own. Make further progress by grasping the fact that there are many possible approaches to the situation—not just "yours" and "theirs." The highest road of all goes through the middle.

Work & Projects

You're overwhelmed by the shadow of the Big Picture. Break the work down into component parts: simple steps you can take one at a time. Focus on what opposing goals have in common . . . how can one solution serve the maximum number of interests?

Guide to Changing Lines

━⊕━ on the First Line

If others are trying to force their will or their way on you, quietly resist. People with good intentions will gently persist; those will selfish interests will move on to easier targets.

━⊕━ on the Second Line

Two people or things which belong together can no longer function as a unit. Take heart; an accidental meeting between the two has potential to restore a good relationship.

━×━ on the Third Line

Though everything seems to be working against you, stick with the person or direction you feel is right. Through your consistency, the matter ends well.

━⊖━ *on the Fourth Line*

You can overcome feelings of loneliness and isolation by seeking out like-minded people who share your passions— and avoid becoming a "lone wolf" in the process.

━x━ *on the Fifth Line*

Others involved are just as sincere as you are. Rip away externals and first impressions; discard assumptions. At the core, you'll find the truth of mutual attraction.

━⊖━ *on the Sixth Line*

You're mistaking good friends for attackers and opponents. To resolve tensions, put aside your strong emotions and focus instead on how others are trying to help you.

Encountering Obstacles

The empowered person sees every obstacle as a challenge: an opportunity to learn something important about the self . . . and also about the nature of life.

Keywords: Effort, breakthrough, victory, persistence, cleverness, flexibility, winning, circumnavigation, triumph

Encourages: Leaping hurdles; studying a situation to find a solution; taking a positive approach to solving problems; approaching difficult situations with eagerness and curiosity; being open to ways over, around, or through stumbling blocks

Cautions against: Retreating from difficulty; insisting that progress should be easy or effortless; focusing on misfortune; interpreting obstacles as "signs I should turn back"; refusing to enlist the help of those who have "been there, done that"

THOUGHT QUESTIONS

What am I supposed to learn from this situation?

How can I go around, through, or over this obstacle with alternative approaches?

Who could help me with this difficulty?

To what extent is this obstacle strictly a matter of my own point of view?

Commentary

When faced with difficulty, too many people panic or whine, blaming others for their circumstances and expecting someone else to rescue them. Empower yourself by shouldering responsibility, analyzing the situation, and pledging to move ahead.

What resources are at hand? What helpful people? What levers might be used to pry this obstacle out of your path? This apparent roadblock may, in fact, be a "school in disguise." What degree will you earn by solving this puzzle?

Love & Relationships

Any obstacle shared is twice as easy to solve. Rather than try to fix things all by yourself, call on the cleverness and resourcefulness of a partner. This cooperative approach shares burdens . . . and changes an obstacle into a transformative experience that binds you closer together.

Work & Projects

Coasting along may seem more fun, however, butting your head against this obstacle is giving you valuable experience that will come in handy in the future. Find ways to enjoy the struggle. Keep a positive outlook, and enlist others in generating unique solutions.

Guide to Changing Lines

━x━ *on the First Line*

Rather than move ahead blindly, stop to analyze this situation. What can you learn by sitting and watching? By listening? By reading further? Before you act, observe.

━x━ *on the Second Line*

In your specific case, duty demands that you break through this obstacle as quickly as possible. Fulfill your obligations; your conduct in difficult times endears you to others.

━●━ *on the Third Line*

Some obstructions aren't challenges—they're signs that we should turn back. Change course now; others will celebrate your return and be thankful for your change of heart.

━x━ *on the Fourth Line*

The best solution to your situation isn't the shortest or easiest one. Make preparations, enlist resources, and insist on the time and support needed to get the job done.

▬x▬ *on the Fifth Line*

Either others are depending on your help, or this challenge is a signpost on the way to your true calling. Either way, persistence attracts helpers and things turn out well.

▬x▬ *on the Sixth Line*

You've gotten past bigger obstacles in the past, and it's tempting to avoid this one entirely. Don't. Helping others is now your duty. Make an alliance and move forward.

40

Maintaining Effort

The empowered person celebrates initial progress, but remains focused, on task, and dedicated to reaching the final goal.

Keywords: Persistence, tenacity, fidelity, faithfulness, doggedness, determination, constancy, perseverance, endurance

Encourages: Sticking with a job to the end; seeing things through; remaining faithful to a cause over long periods of time; being dependable and consistent; building the strength of character required for the long haul; keeping on keeping on; finishing what you start

Cautions against: Being a "fair weather friend"; stepping out "in the middle of things"; abandoning those who need you; being fickle; getting so caught up in initial victory that all emphasis on reaching the final goal is lost; drifting from one half-finished project to the next

THOUGHT QUESTIONS

What milestones remain?

How can I demonstrate my long-term commitment in this situation?

What actions would a consistent, dependable person take now?

How can I preserve the momentum I've achieved so far?

Commentary

Progress begins, and the work of reaching the goal is underway—but the actual achievement of the goal exists purely in the future. Don't mistake the initial easing of tensions and resolution of complication for the final solution.

Restore order and regularity. Tie up loose ends. Ferret out those tasks which linger and bring them to a successful close. Celebrate your progress to date, and convert your optimism and enthusiasm into the fuel you'll need to cross the finish line.

Love & Relationships

You've rounded the corner, but there's still work to be done. If baggage weighs you down, discard it. If lingering ties connect you to someone unhealthy or unsuitable, break them. If saying the unspoken will resolve a matter, then speak up.

Work & Projects

Don't mistake a milestone for the finish line! Rally the troops and focus on making further progress. What steps remain? Revisit schedules, to-do lists, and assignments. Be sure yesterday's plan still applies to today's reality.

Guide to Changing Lines

━x━ *on the First Line*

With obstacles out of the way, it's now time to end the back-slapping and regroup. Take a moment to catch your breath . . . then ask yourself, "What now?"

━⊖━ *on the Second Line*

The key to maintaining your progress so far? Simple, straightforward focus on the basics. Don't be flattered or distracted by accolades; stay the course.

━x━ *on the Third Line*

Making too much of your progress to date will attract unwanted attention from those who might think ill of you. Continue work, but do so without flashiness or fanfare.

━⊖━ *on the Fourth Line*

Celebrations of success will attract people who will fall away once work resumes. Use this time to identify those who will stick with you regardless, and draw closer to them.

━x━ *on the Fifth Line*

Enhancing your success—and changing your world for the better—begins in your own mind. Clarify your goals, outline them clearly, and break away restraining distractions.

━x━ *on the Sixth Line*

In order to make further progress, you must deal with a person or situation that holds you back. Rather than avoid this, it's in your best interest to take decisive action now.

41

Accepting Limits

The empowered person sees the folly in repairing the roof with stones taken from a home's foundation.

Keywords: Boundaries, limitations, restriction, demarcation, range, extent, curtailment, minimums and maximums, barriers

Encourages: Accepting your own limits; embracing the idea that performance and output fluctuate over time; refusing to burn the candle at both ends; setting and sticking to limits; drawing a line and refusing to cross it; enforcing realism and simplicity

Cautions against: Playing the martyr; exhausting yourself in order to serve or support others; working against your own best interests by giving too much of your time, energy, or means; putting on airs; pretending to have money or power you do not possess

THOUGHT QUESTIONS

What are my own personal limits in this situation? How close have I come to them?

How comfortable am I with the idea that I can't do everything?

How can I offer service without exhausting or destroying myself?

What limits or boundaries am I dealing with?

Commentary

Balance is a matter of restriction and limitation; "So far," we say, "and no farther." This approach prevents a blessing—a plentitude of food, for example—from becoming a disruptive curse. Refusing to draw the line somewhere quickly leads to chaos.

This situation calls for you to be aware of your own limits: what you are willing to take, and what you are willing to give. Be honest about these limits, and refuse to act or present yourself in ways that hide or disguise them. In the end, you are who you are.

Love & Relationships

Those people who constantly expect others to be more or less than they really are have strayed onto the path of conditional love. Be honest and frank about limits and realities; don't apologize. Pretense adds stress and invites dishonesty on all sides.

Work & Projects

It's time to take stock of what really is, ignoring, for the moment, what you or the boss would like for reality to be. What has been done, really? What can be done? How realistic are your goals? Any favor earned by unrealistic reports will quickly dissipate.

Guide to Changing Lines

━●━ *on the First Line*

It's good for friends and co-workers to aid each other when their own work is done. Be sure that, in the process, the helpers aren't overextending and exhausting themselves!

━●━ *on the Second Line*

Using yourself up in service to someone else deprives that person of your help in the future and, ultimately, does harm. Pace yourself, and limit your contribution accordingly.

━x━ *on the Third Line*

As personal limits are reached, it's natural for some people to draw closer to us while others move on. Embrace this rhythm; it's part of life. Why pretend otherwise?

━x━ *on the Fourth Line*

Other than those we impose on ourselves, there are very few limits on self-improvement. Transcending some of your self-imposed limits will delight you and your friends.

▬x▬ *on the Fifth Line*

How real are the limits you're dealing with? In some cases—the universe's ability to bestow blessings, for example—there are no limits. How would your situation change if you accepted this?

▬⊖▬ *on the Sixth Line*

Here's an opportunity to prosper—while also making sure others have what they need. There's no limit to the good that right action will achieve for everyone involved.

42

Transcending Limits

The empowered person senses a rare and unique opportunity, and goes above and beyond his or her limits in order to take advantage of it.

Keywords: Growth, bounty, boundlessness, unlimited potential, possibility, potency, development, capability, excellence

Encourages: Going beyond what is expected or accepted; giving more than is asked for; performing above and beyond the call of duty; tapping into the power of the Divine in order to break through a human limit; breaking through boundaries and constraints

Cautions against: Failing to fulfill your greatest potential; accepting less than your own best effort; settling or compromising; hesitating to reach for a dream; refusing to go beyond imagined boundaries; taking a small, dim view of the possible

THOUGHT QUESTIONS

If there were no limits, what would I do?

How open am I to challenges? How intimidated am I by difficulties?

To what extent are the limitations of this situation imagined?

How can I inspire myself to go above and beyond the call of duty?

Commentary

When omens are good and the weather looks fair, only the foolish hesitate to take advantage of the situation. Whatever restrictions have been placed on you are falling away; put this freedom to good use and take action accordingly.

This is a time to tap into your own best potential and enhance your best qualities; it is also a time to shore up shortcomings and transcend anything in your makeup that is less than satisfactory. Act wisely, and you'll find yourself being the very best you can be.

Love & Relationships

A surprising gesture or unselfish act will go a long way in this situation. Break some rules. Do the unexpected. Good energy is on the rise, and you can take advantage of it by refreshing and revitalizing yourself and your relationships in general.

Work & Projects

While the energy is available, get things done. Turn in more work than expected. Beat deadlines. Put in extra work and generate a product of unsurpassed quality. Set new standards for yourself . . . and beat them. This is a time to shine.

Guide to Changing Lines

━⊙━ *on the First Line*

Unlimited energy is available to you, right now, if you'll just tap into it. Clear your mind, focus on what you want, and achieve what you've been longing for.

━x━ *on the Second Line*

Preserve the good energy around you by making sure your motives are pure and your goals selfless. Doing so will extend a run of good luck beyond normal limits.

━x━ *on the Third Line*

You are allowing feelings of guilt and indebtedness to hinder your appreciation for what you've been given. Transcend these limits; take full advantage of what comes your way.

━x━ *on the Fourth Line*

If you're concerned about progress, call on a neutral guide for an assessment of the situation. He will not be limited by your perspective, and can help you see your circumstances with new eyes.

━o━ *on the Fifth Line*

Challenge your own limits with regard to kindness. Go the extra mile. Give more than others request. Be content to be recognized instead of rewarded.

━o━ *on the Sixth Line*

Transcending limits without regard for impact and consequence is an indication that someone is off the best path. Rein this in, or misfortune will follow.

43

Pursuing the Best Course

The empowered person, dedicated to fairness and right action, selects a goal and pursues it with confidence, yet always remains open to better options.

Keywords: Strength, focus, resolution, steadfastness, courageousness, bravery, toughness, firmness, fairness, decisiveness

Encourages: Selecting goals in harmony with our highest values and best character; pursuing those goals with all our heart; refusing to compromise our values or ethics in the name of progress; avoiding and being on the lookout for obstinacy

Cautions against: Mindlessly or dogmatically pressing toward one goal with no regard for ethics or appropriateness; refusing to pay attention to ideas, questions, or assessments other than your own; implementing bad strategy for the sake of consistency

THOUGHT QUESTIONS

How open am I to alternatives, once I choose a direction?

What input or information am I ignoring or overlooking?

How can I make progress while remaining flexible?

What signs would I accept as indicators that I need to adjust my course?

Commentary

Once a breakthrough occurs, we find ourselves swept forward in a rush of welcome movement. We make a mistake, though, if we use this as an excuse to block out any further options for action. Possibilities abound; dismissing them is risky.

The key is to set goals that serve the best and highest purposes, to refuse to compromise our ethics, and to admit the role our own passions play in setting a course. Doing so allows us to admit mistakes, revise our plans, and maximize our own progress.

Love & Relationships

For the moment, forget what you want . . . what's best for all involved? What you imagined or what once served as a goal could change. Are there signs this has happened? If so, it's time to negotiate a new course based on the latest and greatest information.

Work & Projects

Tradition ("What we've always done") and pride ("My way, or the highway!") often prevent people and companies from responding to new situations in clever ways. Think outside the box. What's the shortest possible path from A to B? If you can take it without compromising your ethics and goals . . . it's worth considering.

Guide to Changing Lines

━●━ on the First Line

You're ready for change and forward motion, but the situation is still "sticky" and resistant. Do what you can, gauge your strength, and resist the urge to blunder forward.

━●━ on the Second Line

To succeed, apply greater caution and think several moves ahead. What is likely to happen? How can you prepare for it? Use reason, not emotion, and plot your course.

━●━ on the Third Line

Showing your hand early can complicate your situation. Without compromising your ethics, reserve action for now. This can be lonely, but it allows you to be true to yourself.

━◦━ *on the Fourth Line*

How many times do you have to bang your head against the wall before you see it? When obstacles persist, the universe is telling you something. Don't be stubborn. Change course.

━◦━ *on the Fifth Line*

Evil companions corrupt good morals. As you try to make progress, be sure you don't adopt the unsavory or unethical practices of those you hope to surpass!

━x━ *on the Sixth Line*

Success is imminent, but you must also be on guard against backsliding. In this victory are seeds of loss. Be cautious, re-examine your plan, and avoid any wrongdoing.

44

Resisting Weakness

The empowered person sees heavy objects lifted by strong winds, and understands how those of strong character can be manipulated by subtle, invisible influence.

Keywords: Temptation, appeal, charisma, influence, manipulation, sway, persuasion, denigration, force, bribery, blackmail

Encourages: Holding fast to your ethics; making a conscious effort to be of strong character; understanding your agenda need not be set by those around you; taking care that you influence others for good instead of allowing them to influence you for evil

Cautions against: Allowing those of weak character to persuade you to adopt their methods and perspectives; giving up your dedication to ethics and fairness; slipping

into old and destructive habits; allowing weaker individuals to set your direction for you

THOUGHT QUESTIONS

How certain am I that I am setting, instead of following,
an example?

In what small ways am I being influenced by those around
me?

How might I "take the high road," despite the choices of
others?

To what extent am I swayed by the opinions and values of
others?

Commentary

Having chosen the path of empowerment, we face a constant pressure to abandon our awareness and slip back into
a mindless, unconscious approach to life. How much easier
to allow others to make choices for us! How much easier to
be swept along!

Worse, those with weak character, threatened by the
suggestion that more can be achieved through mindful intention, may try to persuade us to drop our guard and embrace old habits. Surrounded by their influence, we must
be kind, but firm.

Love & Relationships

In any relationship, the two people involved shape and influence each other. Is the stronger influence primarily positive or negative? Especially if you are intent on being your own best self, you must carefully monitor the direction influence flows.

Work & Projects

With so many people dedicated to cutting corners, slacking off, and doing as little as possible, it's all too easy for a good work ethic to be blunted by the bad habits of others. Your best efforts should inspire others; don't allow a lazy mindset to influence you.

Guide to Changing Lines

━×━ *on the First Line*

When confronting a small evil, it's tempting to do nothing. Over time, though, a small evil exerts increasing power and control. Identify it . . . and eliminate it.

━◉━ *on the Second Line*

You'll never eliminate bad influences and temptations, but you can gently shoo them away. Be sure that, in the process, you don't shift them off onto other, weaker people!

━●━ on the Third Line

Back and forth, back and forth. Isn't it time to free your-self of this influence? Until you stand firm against it, you live in constant danger of living under its control.

━●━ on the Fourth Line

We must be in the world, but not of the world. Relation-ships with all kinds of people are necessary, but you must be very careful to monitor the level and direction of influence.

━●━ on the Fifth Line

Holding fast to your highest principles will, eventually, have a positive influence on those around you. No need to preach; just live openly and bravely by your own best ideals.

━●━ on the Sixth Line

Be prepared: some people will actively dislike someone who won't stoop to their level. At the same time, take care that your actions are rooted in strength—never pride.

Building Community

The empowered person observes how small streams form great lakes, and learns a lesson about how communities are made.

Keywords: Connection, bond, family, tribe, clan, society, group, network, congregation, kinship, membership, team

Encourages: Finding people with parallel interests and values; joining a group; becoming part of a larger community; leading or joining a class or organization of like-minded people; volunteering; donating your time, effort, or money to a larger cause

Cautions against: Isolating yourself from others; cutting yourself off from beneficial influences; hoarding your time, energy, or wealth; rejecting friendly overtures;

casting aside the traditions that bind people and families together

THOUGHT QUESTIONS

How involved in the lives of others am I?

How might my influence for good be magnified by joining a group or team?

How much of a team player am I?

To what extent am I integrated into my community?

Commentary

People come together for support and safety: families, churches, cities, corporations. They organize themselves into hierarchies, rallying around leaders, eager to find their own place in a social, political, or religious community. This is natural, and often good.

A position within a community—especially a community organized around a worthy leader for a worthy cause—is comfortable and laudable. Rather than horde all your influence for yourself, consider the value of networking with like-minded folk.

Love & Relationships

Often, a powerful attraction between two people shuts others out. Be as close as you like, but don't forget to find ways to integrate yourself into the larger world. A relationship that shuts out the world may soon find itself cut off from nourishment and energy.

Work & Projects

Working alone limits your contributions. Network. Meet helpful people, and discover what you can do to help them. This isn't manipulative; done in the right spirit, it expands your base of influence, and enables everyone to achieve his or her goals more quickly.

Guide to Changing Lines

━x━ *on the First Line*

A group without a strong leader wavers in its focus and direction. Thinking of joining? Watch the leader. If his words gently direct others, this is a worthy cause.

━x━ *on the Second Line*

Sometimes, coming together doesn't have to be a formal, regimented affair. Embrace simplicity. If currents bring you together with others, accept and celebrate this.

━x━ *on the Third Line*

Established groups can seem, at first, unfriendly to new members. If joining is important to you, request a service position. A lowly start will endear you to the others.

▬⊖▬ *on the Fourth Line*

Rallying people together to meet a higher cause will be more successful than organizing them around one person's appeal. Strive to identify the larger good you're serving.

▬⊖▬ *on the Fifth Line*

Some people join a cause to further it; others join a group hoping to benefit by association. Rather than worry about motivations, focus on getting work done.

▬x▬ *on the Sixth Line*

If your efforts to network prove unsuccessful, keep trying. Be open with others about your needs. In doing so, you'll eventually make the right connection.

46

Pushing Upward

The empowered person observes how a small seedling erupts out of the earth, and learns a lesson about the nature of growth and progress.

Keywords: Work, labor, struggle, attempt, endeavor, exertion, movement, force, effort, exercise, application, attainment, diligence

Encourages: Exerting consistent effort over time; acquiring the resources needed for growth and progress; applying yourself diligently toward a goal; starting small and expanding slowly; taking appropriate action now

Cautions against: Waiting for your goals to come to you; taking a "wait and see" attitude when action would be more appropriate; giving in to a sense of entitlement;

being lazy or unfocused; refusing to apply yourself; coasting along instead of setting a direction

THOUGHT QUESTIONS

Now that the time for action has come, what do I need to be doing?

How can I make best use of this opportunity for growth and progress?

What actions would allow me to look back and say, "I did the right thing!"?

What is the nature of the work I need to do? How can I apply myself to it?

Commentary

Slowly, slowly, a sapling pushes its way out of the ground and becomes a mighty oak. This is the kind of force at work in your situation: a slow but powerful forward motion. Take advantage of it while it lasts, and you can make great progress very easily.

Adapt to obstacles. Now, it's easier than ever to find ways around, over, or through the forces that have confounded you in the past. Meet with mentors, managers, and anyone charged with oversight with confidence. Let "Activity now!" be your motto today.

Love & Relationships

Now is a time for relationships to thrive. Whatever has happened, you must see it as a doorway for growth and opportunity. What small steps can you take today to make the most of the situation? Discuss where you want to go together, and start the journey now.

Work & Projects

There's never been a better time for getting things done. Even obstacles you may meet will quickly become stepping stones to new achievements and opportunities! Use this energy wisely: ask for what you really need, and expect success.

Guide to Changing Lines

▬x▬ on the First Line

Progress is just beginning. Pull strength from your roots and don't be discouraged at all by having to start on the ground floor. Seeds start underground, you know!

▬o▬ on the Second Line

You may not know all the forms and rules, and may have some maturing to do—still, a good attitude and strong work ethic go a long way. Contribute what you can.

━●━ *on the Third Line*

Obstructions fall away! That's good news. Some will wonder when this run of luck will end; for now, though, ignore such thoughts and take advantage of easy progress.

━x━ *on the Fourth Line*

A little hard work today will pay off greatly in the short term! Buckle down, do what needs to be done, and don't worry about reward—it will take care of itself.

━x━ *on the Fifth Line*

With success so close at hand, it's tempting to celebrate—and in celebrating, lose sight of your ultimate goals. Enjoy this lucky time—but remain sober and focused, too.

━x━ *on the Sixth Line*

If you have no clear goal defined, no amount of effort or luck will take you anywhere. Rather than exhaust yourself following impulses, choose a direction first . . . then work.

47

Dealing with Weariness

Rather than be rattled by unavoidable adversity, the empowered person controls all he or she can control in the situation: his or her reaction to it.

Keywords: Exhaustion, oppression, fatigue, brainfog, burnout, debilitation, collapse, heaviness, overwork, droopiness, worn out

Encourages: Maintaining optimism; keeping the faith; focusing on what you really can control; conserving your strength for better times ahead; holding your tongue; accepting what is while also exploring paths to better outcomes

Cautions against: Giving up; allowing weariness to distort your vision of the world; taking rash action just because you're weary; continuing to throw yourself at a hopeless situation; struggling against the inevitable

THOUGHT QUESTIONS

What can I really control in this situation?

How do I react to adversity? How profitable is that response?

To what extent am I willing to give up control and take what comes?

How can I refresh myself, despite the situation?

Commentary

Adversity will break the weak; the strong, however, bend with the wind, creating the momentum that will allow them to snap back when the storm has passed. Rather than try to seize control, the wise person keeps his or her eyes on the goal and persists.

If we are willing to accept success, we must also accept times of adversity. Such times wear us down, and there's no harm in admitting when we're tired and frustrated. Now is the time to conserve strength. Hunker down, or take small steps. Things will improve.

Love & Relationships

Every relationship has its ups and downs, peaks and valleys. This is a low point; if you value the relationship, take a deep breath. Say less, and observe more. Success is still possible, if you both really want it . . . so take time to define what you really want.

Work & Projects

Divorced from our goals, work becomes drudgery. Assess the extent to which this work gets you closer to your goals, and act accordingly. In the meantime, just keep putting one foot in front of the other, one day at a time, and keep a level head about you.

Guide to Changing Lines

━x━ *on the First Line*

Now is the time to tap your reservoir of inner strength. Rather than sit and sulk, get out and do something—anything!—to help you restore a sense of balance and stability.

━⊖━ *on the Second Line*

While things look fine on the outside, inside, you're in turmoil. Prayer, meditation, or simple downtime will help. To prepare for better times, start by stabilizing yourself.

━x━ *on the Third Line*

To some extent, our feelings are chosen; is it possible that you're making this situation feel worse (and therefore be worse) than it really is? Clear your mind, and be decisive.

━●━ on the Fourth Line

Concerns over how others will react to your wishes and goals hold you back. You're strong-natured, though; if you're true to yourself, real friends will celebrate your progress.

━●━ on the Fifth Line

While now it seems no one is around to help you, better times are close at hand. Prepare for the upturn with meditation, prayer, or stillness. Compose yourself and hang in there.

━x━ on the Sixth Line

To what extent are your difficulties a "cage of your own making?" Don't be ruled by fear and hesitation. Change your attitude, make a choice, and things will improve.

48

Tapping Potential

The empowered person sees water being drawn from a well and understands that an unlimited source of strength and refreshment lies deep within.

Keywords: Inner resources, inner strength, capability, ability, promise, aptitude, skill, forte, imagination, genius, prowess, competency

Encourages: Helping yourself and others achieve a personal best; drawing on internal reserves to do the apparently impossible; finding your own best path; doing what you were meant to do; applying yourself to achieve more than you dare to dream

Cautions against: Changing superficial details instead of working on the more important internal issues; expending your energy on work that fails to satisfy you;

careless application of effort in ways that exhaust but do not lead to achievement; busywork

THOUGHT QUESTIONS

To what extent am I doing the work I feel "called" to do?

What is my distinctive "gift" or genius? How can I apply it now?

What am I doing to refresh my inner supply of creativity and energy?

How can I tap into my highest creative powers? Into the Divine?

Commentary

A properly tended well can supply water to a city for centuries. If proper care is taken—if the city doesn't overtax or poison it, for example—the well may contribute to the lives of millions of people. In this way, a well becomes a symbol for abundance and life.

Your inner reserve of strength and energy is also inexhaustible—if you take care to replenish and honor it. How are you feeding your spirit and creative soul? How closely do you listen to your own inner wisdom? How are you applying your strengths to better life for you and for others?

Love & Relationships

You can't give to someone else energy and creativity that you don't possess. Revitalize and refresh your relationship by taking some time for personal growth. You become a better partner when you invest some time in your own growth and development.

Work & Projects

You're a great worker, but you have to be careful to take care of yourself. A broken bucket can't draw anything from the well; tend to your own needs to avoid this unfortunate situation. Get in touch with your roots and rediscover your real potential.

Guide to Changing Lines

▬x▬ on the First Line

To what extent are you throwing away your energy? Rather than waste your time and effort, find a project or relationship that is deserving of what you have to give.

▬o▬ on the Second Line

You have great strengths and wonderful qualities, but you're neglecting them, and they're in danger of atrophy. Find work and friends who challenge you to be your best possible self.

▬o▬ on the Third Line

Resources are available to you, but they aren't being tapped! This is a shame. Make sure you're positioned to take advantage of the best that you (and others) have to offer.

▬x▬ *on the Fourth Line*

Some downtime for self-improvement isn't a waste of time—it's an investment in the future. Rest. Doing so will make you more valuable to others later on.

▬⊝▬ *on the Fifth Line*

What you have to offer can only benefit the world if you make it known. Don't be shy about exposing your best qualities or offering to help. Share what you can do.

▬x▬ *on the Sixth Line*

You're in a position to make a huge difference in your life and the lives of others. Open yourself to the spirit of abundance. Accept offers, lend a hand, and help anyone who asks.

49

Transforming Yourself

The empowered person observes how animals adapt to their environment and learns a lesson about thriving in the midst of constant change.

Keywords: Change, metamorphosis, conversion, alteration, improvement, shift in thinking, transition, modification, reinvention

Encourages: Recognizing the necessity and value of change; discarding outmoded ways of thinking or acting; surprising or delighting yourself by starting a new enterprise or effort; observing change with an eye toward attuning yourself to its rhythms

Cautions against: Resisting change; clamoring for a return to the old ways; honoring tradition to the point you limit your ability to respond to current issues; sticking with the "same old, same old"; balking at opportunities to step outside your comfort zone

THOUGHT QUESTIONS

If I were not constrained by expectations and history, what would I do?

What is the next step in my personal evolution?

What changes in thought or action would allow me to succeed?

How can I "break the mold" and do something out of character?

Commentary

We tend to be creatures of habit; as a result, we're challenged when times, seasons, and situations change. What worked before won't necessarily work today; the person we were yesterday may not be equipped to thrive in the world of tomorrow.

Understanding this, empowered people attune themselves to opportunities for reinvention. Rather than dread change, they see new circumstances as new springboards for success. Rather than dream of the good old days . . . they create the good old *now*.

Love & Relationships

You are constantly evolving and changing; as a result, your relationship is changing, too. You aren't the same people you were when you met. Seize on this as an opportunity for growth, and you'll grow closer together. Who do the two of you need to be today?

Work & Projects

If you continue bringing yesterday's strategies to today's challenges, you'll be doomed to repeat the past . . . or, worse, you'll limit success by limiting options. Start from scratch. How would you approach this challenge if you had unlimited resources?

Guide to Changing Lines

━●━ *on the First Line*

Before initiating change, be sure you know where you are (how else will you be able to monitor progress?). Take stock of the present before lunging toward the future.

━x━ *on the Second Line*

Change is desperately needed now, but before launching a program of revolution, be sure you are prepared. Line up resources, support systems, and like-minded helpers.

━●━ *on the Third Line*

Rather than rush toward revolution, ask yourself, "Is there really a need for change?" Watch and listen for three signs of needed change. If you don't see them, then wait.

▬⊖▬ *on the Fourth Line*

Any changes you make must be supported by a higher authority, or they will be blocked before you begin. Check your motives and enlist the aid and enthusiasm of others.

▬⊖▬ *on the Fifth Line*

The time is especially ripe for forward movement and change—and you can sense it. Why are you sitting here? Take advantage of the moment and get going.

▬x▬ *on the Sixth Line*

Massive change may not be possible just now. Change what you can: yourself. Others will be impacted, and some degree of transformation will follow.

Embracing Your Calling

Just as a pot fulfills its ultimate purpose by containing a tasty stew, the empowered person strives to do what he or she was meant to do.

Keywords: Vocation, profession, career, challenge, mission, purpose, design, intention, destiny, fate, direction

Encourages: Following your dream; doing what you do best without regard for reward or payment; turning control of your life over to a higher power; accepting the work you are best suited to do; moving away from busy-work to work you find meaningful

Cautions against: Making changes in vocation just for the sake of variety; moving from one dead-end job to another; allowing your life to be guided by chance instead of intention; living life without a sensitivity to pattern and purpose

THOUGHT QUESTIONS

What am I uniquely suited to do? What can only I make happen?

What am I doing to get in touch with what divinity has in store for me?

How can I discover my own best path?

What guides my life? How successful is this arrangement so far?

Commentary

A handcrafted bowl in a museum display loses its facility and becomes a work of art—something to be studied, but no longer used. You must resist being assigned the same status in your life. Usefulness and finding true purpose is more important than being put on display.

Submerged in the noise and chaos of the everyday world, you may have difficulty isolating your true mission. Be still. Open your heart. What work calls you?

Love & Relationships

Some people seem meant to be together; others are together for reasons of convenience or practicality. You must make the choice that's right for you . . . but you should also remember that you deserve a relationship that feeds you and helps you evolve.

Work & Projects

Every minute spent working on projects that are not re-
lated to your larger goals is wasted time. Rather than bank
hours and hours of effort that you'll eventually regret, why
not focus more energy on shifting your path toward your
true calling?

Guide to Changing Lines

━x━ *on the First Line*

Every good person can, in some way, succeed. Success, ultimately, is a matter of finding your unique contribution
and making it, no matter how large or how small.

━⊖━ *on the Second Line*

As you work to find your true purpose, be proud of your
accomplishments. If you emphasize what you have actually done, then no one can accuse you of bragging.

━⊖━ *on the Third Line*

You may find yourself in a situation where, despite having
much to offer, you are not recognized. Focus on your potential. Wait. Your time is coming soon.

━⊖━ *on the Fourth Line*

Associating with weak people who are not on their own
best path may limit your ability to find your own. How can
you succeed if others around you are pulling you down?

▬x▬ *on the Fifth Line*

Despite success, remain approachable. Modesty goes a long way; in fact, it will draw helpful people to you, who will, in turn, increase your success.

▬o▬ *on the Sixth Line*

When offering insights, do so with firmness and purity. When asking for insight, be true to your goals, but open to new possibilities and direction. Otherwise . . . why ask?

Handling a Crisis

The empowered person may initially jump at a thunder-clap . . . but in its wake, he or she recovers enough presence of mind to come in out of the storm.

Keywords: Decisive action, focus, concentration, coolness, calmness, centeredness, clarity, contingency planning, reaction, response

Encourages: Maintaining a cool head; keeping your wits about you; having a Plan B and Plan C; dealing with what is instead of what was supposed to be; keeping your chin up; making hard decisions quickly and efficiently; responding instead of reacting

Cautions against: Running amok; being startled into action; allowing fear to rule your responses to crisis; giving panic free rein; being taken in by fear tactics; being unprepared for an emergency; beating yourself up for momentarily losing balance

THOUGHT QUESTIONS

What really scares me? How will I deal with it, should the circumstance arise?

What calming ritual could I adopt that would allow me to see clearly in a crisis?

How thoroughly have I planned for contingencies?

How can I help keep others calm during the worst of times?

Commentary

A loud noise and a sudden flash will make almost anyone jump. The key is recovery: moving past the initial, reflexive reaction, marshaling your critical faculties, and responding with reason (instead of panic). Good leaders learn this lesson early.

Every sane person experiences some fear; your goal, then, is not developing immunity to fear, but evolving sophisticated techniques for dealing productively with it. Knowing your own goals and values, being centered, and focusing on action is a good start.

Love & Relationships

In terms of this relationship, what's your worst fear? How will you deal with this situation, should it arise? Discussing these things can be uncomfortable at first, but can make you stronger in the long run. Meanwhile: keep a cool head, whatever the situation.

Work & Projects

Stay calm, and maintain perspective. To what extent is this a life-and-death situation? From a broader point of view, is this crisis all it's cracked up to be . . . or is this just another corporate fire drill? Maintain an even keel, and you'll weather the storm.

Guide to Changing Lines

━●━ on the First Line

At first, this ordeal will seem overwhelming and threatening, but in retrospect, it's a growth experience. With time, you'll see the pattern of events in an entirely new light.

━x━ on the Second Line

The current crisis may threaten great personal loss. Accept this; the losses are not permanent, and what you lose today will effortlessly return to you in the short term.

━x━ on the Third Line

A momentary pause in the face of sudden crisis is understandable; now, however, it's time to rouse yourself and take action. Set emotions aside and do what needs doing.

▬⊙▬ *on the Fourth Line*

Strong emotions threaten your ability to deal effectively with this crisis. Stop. Take a deep breath. Chat with a mentor or friend. Focus before attempting forward motion.

▬x▬ *on the Fifth Line*

You face an onslaught of several crises, one after another, with little time for recovery. No overwhelming loss will come, however, so steel yourself and resolve to move forward with courage and determination.

▬x▬ *on the Sixth Line*

The shock of crisis is still so fresh, you've not been able to recover. Keep still. Others will urge premature action; reserve your right to wait until you feel calm and centered.

Being in the Moment

Though the outside world becomes a chaotic whirlwind of action and emotion, the empowered person marshals his thoughts, focuses energy, and acts accordingly.

Keywords: Stillness, meditation, focus, presence of mind, contemplation, thoughtfulness, musing, mental clarity, right action

Encourages: Alternating between meditation and action as needed; practicing calming breath techniques; finding your center; choosing to live outside the grip of fear and dizzy activity; listening to calming music; making the most of the now

Cautions against: Getting caught up in the chaos of events; allowing your mind to flitter from one subject to the next; confusing yourself with the confusion around you;

meditation at the expense of action; action without reflection

THOUGHT QUESTIONS

How can I clear my mind and find my center?

What strategies would allow me to feel a greater degree of calmness and control?

How can I move quickly from contemplation to right action?

To what extent am I able to put worry and regret aside?

Commentary

Popular meditation practice focuses exclusively on stillness. This can be impractical, as life requires action. The empowered person lives in a state of balanced reflection, but is also able to maintain this state of mind while taking action in the real world.

Keeping your balance is frequently a matter of being in the moment. What needs to be done right now, today? Avoid worrying about what might happen or what has happened; take care of what needs to be done now, and you will enjoy great success. Small steps!

Love & Relationships

Let worry, fear, and concern drop away. What does your partner or friend need at this moment? Be guided by a sense of the present—not by fears rooted in the past or the future. Enjoy what is; if what is falls short of your dreams, revise your reality.

Work & Projects

Rather than worry about the big deadline, focus on what can be done today. Rather than worry about finishing, determine to work with focus and mindfulness for the next thirty minutes. You'll get more done this way, and amaze yourself with the progress you make.

Guide to Changing Lines

━x━ *on the First Line*

Most mistakes are made in the initial rush to action. Halt, reflect, and then take action. If you're already underway, stop now, get your bearings, and beware of "drift."

━x━ *on the Second Line*

Be aware of the role you play in the plans of others. Unless you stand up for yourself, you may discover you've been pressed into a service you'd rather not perform.

━●━ *on the Third Line*

You can't force relaxation and focus! Sitting rigidly or beating your mind into submission are unrealistic approaches. Sit. Breathe. Let go. Do this several minutes a day and succeed.

━x━ *on the Fourth Line*

One key to peace is to quench the mind's tendency to worry about things from a selfish perspective. Imagine you're taken care of. Now—what remains to be done?

━x━ *on the Fifth Line*

There's a temptation afoot to focus more on talk than on action. Reserve words. Let your actions reveal the intentions of your heart, and you'll have nothing to be sorry for.

━●━ *on the Sixth Line*

Your efforts to calm yourself and take a more reflective approach will prove effective. Continue with a mindful, balanced strategy, and you'll enjoy great success.

53

Taking Things Slowly

The empowered person observes the slow transformation of an acorn into a mighty oak, and learns a lesson about the value of gradual progress over time.

Keywords: Gentle action, deceleration, deliberateness, slowness, moderation, relaxation, decompression, gradual progress

Encourages: Achieving gradual growth; pacing yourself; taking a leisurely pace; stopping to smell the roses; scaling your response and activity over time; allowing slow, natural growth to come about in its own time; embodying patience; taking the long-term view

Cautions against: Forcing sudden change; disrupting the natural cycle of growth by rushing progress; skipping critical steps; thinking a quick change in the situation will have a lasting effect; applying quick fixes when deep changes are needed

THOUGHT QUESTIONS

How does my current strategy fit in to my long-term strategy?

To what extent am I allowing for slow, positive change over time?

How realistic are my expectations, given the maturity of the situation?

To what extent do I depend on quick fixes instead of real "cures"?

Commentary

Some things can't be hurried. Trees don't spring up over night. Great wine takes time. Personal growth, too, is a matter of dedication over time. Beginners clamor for instant results, not understanding that anything easily achieved is also easily lost.

Take a long-term approach. Pace yourself. There's no real hurry; much of the push to action exists in your own mind. Be kind to yourself, and give yourself permission to move according to your own pace. (What pace can you realistically embrace, other than your own?)

Love & Relationships

No one but you can set the standard for where a relationship is going, and how fast it gets there. Rush things, and you'll exhaust the relationship prematurely; drag your feet, and you'll retard its growth. Let go; let the relationship set its own pace, and enjoy what is.

Work & Projects

Divide the remaining work into small portions that you can do each day. Set and meet this quota, and the work won't seem overwhelming at all. Also, beware the temptation to force new and unskilled people to perform to mature standards. Scale all expectations.

Guide to Changing Lines

━x━ on the First Line

When starting out, you very naturally move more slowly than you would otherwise. Ignore criticism. Find your pace. There's no blame in making your own way.

━x━ on the Second Line

Your development has progressed to the point that you're ready to take action. Do so, and, as you find out interesting things, maintain peace by sharing with others.

━⊖━ *on the Third Line*

By struggling to enforce your own timetable on this situation, you have jeopardized your chances for success. Maintain your position, but embrace natural development from this point forward.

━x━ *on the Fourth Line*

Having trouble finding firm ground to stand on? You'll do better if you embrace some options you've discarded or tend to ignore. Temper progress with flexibility.

━⊖━ *on the Fifth Line*

The criteria being used to judge progress need revision. Work past bad assumptions and get back in touch with what really matters, and you can still succeed.

━⊖━ *on the Sixth Line*

Work nears completion, though remnants from this situation linger and may play a useful role in future events. Learn from mistakes, and become an example to others.

54

Managing Relationships

The empowered person knows the value of sincere affection, and takes action to protect relationships of all kinds from abuse and neglect.

Keywords: Rapport, affinity, kinship, liaison, confidence, symbiosis, mutuality, trust, bonding, connection, alliance, due diligence

Encourages: Taking measures to keep relationships of all kinds healthy and functional; maintaining friendships; working toward stable, long-term relationships; adjusting your relationship to deal effectively with the demands of the time; showing affection

Cautions against: Placing unreasonable demands on others; indulging selfish motives; tainting a good relationship with selfish or unreasonable demands; allowing an inappropriate amount of time to lapse between meetings; failing to follow up

THOUGHT QUESTIONS

How mindful am I of the value of my relationships?

What can I do to demonstrate the value I place on true friends and partners?

When a relationship has been neglected, what can I do to repair it?

In a given relationship, what can I do to keep my motives and actions pure?

Commentary

The stability of any voluntary relationship between people hinges on mutual respect and benefit. This does not mean we should think in terms of using people; instead, it merely points out that in healthy relationships, each person gains something.

Relationships must be evaluated with the end in mind. Where is this relationship taking you? Navigating temporary setbacks and disagreements is easier when you keep the ultimate purpose of the relationship in mind. Be sure your direction is defined by intention!

Love & Relationships

Romantic relationships and friendships are always alliances of choice; that's why it's so important to keep an eye on both the quality and equality of the arrangement. Now's a good time to check in and make sure everyone involved is getting what he or she needs.

Work & Projects

Work relationships can be very difficult to manage, because progress must continue despite personal agendas and perceptions. Do what you can to keep the peace, and focus on getting things done. Avoid unhealthy habits, including gossip and backbiting.

Guide to Changing Lines

━●━ on the First Line

A good relationship hinges on compromise. Everyone involved must be comfortable with occasionally playing "second fiddle." To what extent are you comfortable with this?

━●━ on the Second Line

If we value a good relationship, we allow the value we assign to it to govern our behavior even when the others involved in it are not around to watch us. Act accordingly.

▬x▬ *on the Third Line*

Your friendships and relationships tend to be hampered by a tendency to demand too much in terms of aid and support. This can damage self-esteem. Strive for equity.

▬⊖▬ *on the Fourth Line*

You can't rush the formation of a good relationship. Don't smother others; instead, allow things to develop naturally. You'll build higher quality relationships as a result.

▬x▬ *on the Fifth Line*

Struggles over who outranks whom and who holds the most authority are pointless. Accept your friends for who they are, and encourage them to do the same for you.

▬x▬ *on the Sixth Line*

Some people are our friends by intent; others, we associate with purely as a matter of habit. Beware a relationship that fulfills forms, but does little for the soul.

Having It All

The empowered person sees a time of abundance and thinks of the noonday sun: warm, bright, luxurious—but also beginning its daily decline.

Keywords: Affluence, wealth, plenty, fertility, abundance, luxury, opulence, profusion, lushness, bountifulness

Encourages: Making hay while the sun shines; reveling in achievements; taking advantage of supreme good fortune while preparing for change; being grateful for blessings; taking action while energies are at their most positive

Cautions against: Wasting a perfect opportunity; believing that a time of great luck, energy, and progress will last forever; hoarding the fruits of productivity and refusing to deploy them for the good of all; disregarding all potential for change or downturn

THOUGHT QUESTIONS

While I can have whatever I want ... what do I really want?

How can I best channel these blessings so their impact lasts as long as possible?

To what extent am I prepared for the inevitable decline that must occur?

How can I best celebrate and experience the fullness of luxury and plenty?

Commentary

Celebrate! You are positioned to achieve almost anything, if your actions are right and your character beyond reproach. This is a time of plenty; make the most of it by accepting what comes and reaching for whatever bounty comes your way.

The sun has risen, and now is the time of brightest noon. Some say it's pessimistic to speak of a coming sunset now; the wise, however, note this is only realistic. Change is the only constant. Keep this in mind, and you'll never fail to make best use of this time.

Love & Relationships

This is a potentially golden time, when the two of you can achieve much if you work together. Set differences aside, make investments, spruce up the house, and make time to enjoy each other. Success is virtually unlimited if you work toward mutual goals today.

Work & Projects

Your potential for success is virtually unlimited today. Push past obstacles, break through resistance, and put your plans in motion. The resources you need will fall into your hands. Revel in this easy progress; this window of opportunity won't always be open.

Guide to Changing Lines

━●━ *on the First Line*

Take double advantage of this time of prosperity and energy by partnering with someone of like mind. Enhance success by including others in your plans for progress.

━×━ *on the Second Line*

Jealousy and bickering obstruct your ability to take best advantage of this time. Discuss your plans openly with others in order to win support and amplify your success.

━●━ *on the Third Line*

Others with less strength of character and skill are already taking advantage of this time. They're in the lead, and grab all the glory. Don't fret. Your time will come around again.

━●━ *on the Fourth Line*

While the path to success is obstructed by the actions of others, you have a resource on hand that complements your efforts and allows you to move ahead. Use it.

▬×▬ *on the Fifth Line*

Before moving ahead, get advice. Talk with a mentor or trusted friend. This person will give you good counsel. Take it, and your success will be greatly amplified.

▬×▬ *on the Sixth Line*

Pride goes before a fall! Hogging glory, credit, and payoff results in a setback. Moving forward at any price leads to disaster. Revise your approach and attitude now.

Crossing Unfamiliar Territory

In unfamiliar situations, the empowered person is confident enough to play the humble role of learner and observer.

Keywords: Trailblazers, pioneers, wanderers, sightseers, sojourners, visitors, newbies, tourists, fish out of water, travelers, beginners

Encourages: Learning from those with more experience; observing to see how something gets done; asking for directions; using previous experience to make sense of the present; accepting guidance and advice; blazing a new trail after getting the best information

Cautions against: Causing strife by disregarding local customs; breaking laws or sowing discord out of ignorance; blundering forward when watching quietly would be the better strategy; refusing to accept the value of the experience of others

THOUGHT QUESTIONS

How open am I to suggestions, advice, direction, and guidance?

How much value do I place on the experience of others?

How can I learn as much as possible about this new situation?

To what extent am I comfortable playing the openly ignorant student?

Commentary

At some point, everything is new to everyone, so there's no harm in admitting ignorance or being uninformed. Watch and learn. Wherever your travels take you (literally or metaphorically), adopt the language, clothing, and customs of the locals. Blend in.

A good beginner asks questions, welcomes input, and accepts direction with gratitude. Disaster awaits those who, refusing to expose their own ignorance, make a pretense of experience and knowledge. You can't fool people who matter; so why try?

Love & Relationships

A relationship, by its nature, is always expanding into new territory. Travel with confidence and caution. Ask questions. Don't assume knowledge on your part or your partner's part. Communicate freely, and admit what you can't do or don't know.

Work & Projects

A pretense of professionalism is easy to project in the short term, but impossible to maintain. If you're confused, ask questions. If you lack something, ask for it. Provide higher-ups with frank assessments, and always serve up problems with solutions on the side.

Guide to Changing Lines

▬x▬ on the First Line

Preserve your reputation and dignity by humbly accepting whatever help comes your way. Don't put up a front or use humor to hide ignorance. Be open and learn.

▬x▬ on the Second Line

If you keep in touch with who you are and where you're going, unfamiliar territory isn't very threatening. Humble confidence draws aid to you; right action elicits help.

━⊖━ *on the Third Line*

Loud, rude misbehavior (including nosiness and arrogance) has cost you much in this situation. You're currently on your own. To turn things around, apologize and mean it.

━⊖━ *on the Fourth Line*

This situation is in flux. You are safe and stable, but the potential for loss remains, and that's why you feel uneasy. Wait for the situation to change before taking action.

━x━ *on the Fifth Line*

To succeed in a new situation, learn the rules and conform to them. This makes a good first impression, which will win you friends and supporters.

━⊖━ *on the Sixth Line*

You're in danger of becoming someone who adapts to new challenges with difficulty. Rather than continue in pride and arrogance, sober up. Strive for flexibility.

Exerting Subtle Influence

The empowered person observes how invisible winds carve desert rocks, and learns an important lesson about the value of gradual pressure applied consistently over time.

Keywords: Nuance, subtleness, refinement, hints, insinuations, subliminals, innuendos, gradual change

Encourages: Dropping hints; sending small reminders; breaking a large request into several smaller, stepped requests; setting a consistent example for others to follow; approaching a problem by breaking it down into small, bite-sized chunks

Cautions against: Attempting to change minds and hearts by force; expecting too much change too soon; breaking a relationship by exerting inappropriate control; trying to do too much at once; ordering others to think or feel a certain way

THOUGHT QUESTIONS

How persistent am I?

How can I be more subtle in my approach?

To what extent am I in this for the long haul?

How can I slowly bring others around to my perspective?

Commentary

Over centuries, a persistent drop of water will drill holes in the hardest of rocks. In the same way, a persistent, consistent approach to your problem will slowly yield progress over time. The key? Scaling your effort for the long haul.

Don't expect movement or success today . . . or even tomorrow. Instead, embody the highest principles of your own best self—a process that will slowly persuade others of the value of your approach. Sudden motion frightens people; persistence pays.

Love & Relationships

You're expecting too much, too soon, if you expect this situation to change suddenly. If you possess the patience to engineer gradual change over time, have at it. If you're in a hurry, your efforts would be better applied elsewhere.

Work & Projects

Slow and steady wins the race. This change will take time to engineer, and perhaps even longer to implement. Don't expect mastery in minutes; instead, be gentle with your-self and others. Lead by example, and others will eventu-ally catch on.

Guide to Changing Lines

▬x▬ *on the First Line*

There's a difference between gentleness and indecision. Gentle pressure achieves results only when applied toward a consistent goal over a long period of time. Waver, and all is lost.

▬⊖▬ *on the Second Line*

You're not the only person who is trying to influence this situation. Trace things back to their roots, and surprising new information will come to light.

▬⊖▬ *on the Third Line*

Thinking about this any further amounts to beating a dead horse. Take action already! Any further deliberation is just doubt in disguise.

▬x▬ *on the Fourth Line*

Responsibility and experience have combined to make you especially well-suited for this task. Apply gentle influ-ence, and great success is assured.

➖ *on the Fifth Line*

Things didn't start well, but you are well-positioned to make revisions and secure progress. Begin with careful planning and reflection, then make the changes needed.

➖ *on the Sixth Line*

You know enough to know that ill will has ruined this situation. Rather than head toward confrontation, back off. Further progress will only bring you pain.

58

Interacting with Others

The empowered person observes the expansion of a lake, and concludes that getting constant input is one key to consistent, healthy growth.

Keywords: Interaction, expression, sharing, discourse, discussion, dialogue, reciprocation, interchange, exchange, conversation

Encourages: Joining a community of like-minded people; sharing ideas and expertise; attending conventions; illustrating your point in appropriate ways; adopting and practicing a new idea or approach; getting input from as many people as possible

Cautions against: Being a lone wolf; refusing to offer up your conclusions for criticism or input; avoiding association; placing inadequate value on what others have to offer; drawing a circle that shuts people out; pushing others away

THOUGHT QUESTIONS

To what extent am I in regular contact with like-minded others?

How can I expand my circle of friends and mentors?

How can I show others that I'm open to their company and advice?

What input or counsel am I rejecting or neglecting?

Commentary

A natural lake, fed constantly by springs, maintains its level or perhaps even grows over time. A man-made lake, cut off from fresh water, will eventually evaporate. People, too, need constant stimulation and fresh interaction in order to preserve their vitality.

For humans, friends, co-workers, mentors, and a community of like-minded people provide a stimulus for growth. Our interaction with others brings us joy, and offers the opportunity to amplify the good in our life by sharing that good with others.

Love & Relationships

If unpartnered, now is a good time to actively seek a person—or a community of people—who can help you explore your emotional and sensitive side. If partnered, consider finding a larger community of people who share your and your partner's interests.

Work & Projects

Joining a professional association or finding a local group of people in your field is wise, as it builds your network of contacts and exposes you to fresh ideas. In the meantime, now is a good time to get outside opinions on any work in progress.

Guide to Changing Lines

━⊖━ on the First Line

Increase your appeal to others by expressing your contentment with life. Offer your own unique self, without putting on airs, and seek nothing in return.

━⊖━ on the Second Line

Some of your associates indulge in practices or viewpoints that, if adopted, hinder your development and happiness. Tolerate others, but hold fast to your personal standards.

━×━ on the Third Line

Unless you feed your soul with good friends and right action, you'll be too easily distracted by the shallow prattle of the world. What can be set aside?

━⊖━ *on the Fourth Line*

A continued debate or protracted decision eats away at your contentment. Allow your values to steer you toward the higher road, and ensure peace.

━⊖━ *on the Fifth Line*

Negative influences seek to pull you away from your path. Rather than indulge these people, recognize the situation and take measures to protect yourself.

━x━ *on the Sixth Line*

Giving in to flattery or going along with the crowd will not bring you the results you desire. Set your own course. Keep your own counsel. Find friends who build you up.

59

Achieving Unity

The empowered person recognizes the role of ego in creating barriers and dividing people, and determines that he or she will set ego aside.

Keywords: Focus, balance, solidarity, oneness, integrity, wholeness, completeness, integration, reintegration, togetherness, harmony

Encourages: Meditating; acting in selfless ways; participating in religious or spiritual practice with the goal of self-improvement; enjoying fellowship with other people; seeking an experience of the Divine; participating fully in your faith

Cautions against: Practicing spiritual isolation; overemphasizing your own wants, needs, and desires; being pulled in several directions at once by "the ten thousand things"; allowing pride or greed to sway your decisions and actions

THOUGHT QUESTIONS

How quiet is my mind? To what degree am I in control of my thoughts?

To what extent do I enjoy a "oneness" of purpose?

How do I express my spiritual side? How can this be enhanced?

How can I combine the mundane and mystical aspects of my life?

Commentary

Unity is a spiritual concept. On a personal level, unity of spirit allows us to identify and pursue a consistent mission. It infuses our sense of ethics and helps us set our values. Unifying yourself—achieving clarity and consistency—will have dramatic impact.

On a communal level, unity is a matter of fellowship: active participation in shared goals. There is a need to identify and focus on what everyone involved has in common. Use this to build the understanding and trust that transforms strangers into a community.

Love & Relationships

At its very best, a relationship produces unity. Those involved don't have to be identical in their tastes and appearance, but they should share, at a minimum, a sense of where they're going together. To what extent does this unity exist in your relationship?

Work & Projects

Large projects require the coordination of many different people, applying their skills and talents toward a single goal. Be wary of opportunities for fragmentation and dissolution. Bring people together regularly for progress checks and input sessions. Focus!

Guide to Changing Lines

▬x▬ *on the First Line*

Disunity is brewing, threatening future progress. Take action now to identify misunderstandings and provide resolution, or pay the price later on.

▬⊙▬ *on the Second Line*

You are becoming aware of tendencies that push you away from others. Take action now to break down these walls, improve your outlook, and extend fellowship to other people.

▬x▬ *on the Third Line*

You're so caught up in the situation, you have given yourself completely over to it. For the moment, this is fine, and some self-sacrifice will serve you well.

▬x▬ *on the Fourth Line*

Your actions influence many people, including some who are not in your closest personal circle. Be sure to act with fairness. Do what is genuinely best for everyone involved.

▬⊖▬ *on the Fifth Line*

Watch for the arrival of a great idea, which will serve as a unifying force. This will focus energy, restore direction, and move you past misunderstandings.

▬⊖▬ *on the Sixth Line*

A need arises for you to take action on behalf of those you hold most dear. Unify your "family" by protecting them or acting in their best interests.

60

Setting Limits

The empowered person observes the destruction created by a flooded river, and concludes that limits play an important role in a balanced life.

Keywords: Boundaries, barriers, self-discipline, restriction, regulation, parameters, definition, constraints, quotas, enclosure, exclusion

Encourages: Being thrifty; sticking to a diet; honoring your budget; refusing to compromise your ethics or goals; drawing the line; enforcing discipline; controlling destructive impulses; insulating yourself from distraction

Cautions against: Being a spendthrift; spending more than you make; breaking the rules; going overboard; cheating on your diet; allowing others (or yourself!) to revel in unhealthy excesses; going berserk; losing control.

THOUGHT QUESTIONS

How might life improve if I observed some healthy self-limitation?

What areas of life do I struggle to control?

What is my weakness? How might limits aid me in dealing with it?

How can I know when the time comes to "rein things in?"

Commentary

Without limits, chaos rules. Even when circumstances would support a little license, a conservative approach can be useful. Living within your limits during times of plenty makes it easier to live within your limits when the going gets tough.

Limits that go too far build resentment (even limits have their limits!), but appropriate limitation provides structure and stability. Voluntary limits, self-imposed limits, and limitations prescribed by duty define us as people and fortify our character.

Love & Relationships

Healthy relationships depend on limits: limits you set for your own behavior, limits you place on a partner's behavior, and limits you agree to as a couple. Know the rules, and insist that they be honored. If undefined, take action now to define them.

Work & Projects

When the situation threatens to overwhelm you or tip over into chaos, you experience the need for limits. Draw some lines. Set standards. Insist that these be met. Now is the time to say, "This far, and no further."

Guide to Changing Lines

━●━ *on the First Line*

Obstacles can be limits in disguise. Take an objective look at the situation. Do you know when to stop? Obeying limits builds energy; railing against them depletes you.

━●━ *on the Second Line*

As obstacles fall away, you're being given a sign that now is the time for action. Set deliberation aside, focus on your goals, and proceed with confidence.

━x━ *on the Third Line*

Refusing to limit yourself will force you to confront an inflexible fact of life: actions have consequences. Don't blame others; strengthen yourself by enforcing limits now.

━x━ *on the Fourth Line*

You can save time and effort by putting limitations to work for you. Discover the "rules" that govern your situation, and use your cleverness to play them to your advantage.

━●━ *on the Fifth Line*

Set a good example by applying limits to yourself first, and then to others. Laying down the law for others while remaining unrestricted builds resentment and discord.

━x━ *on the Sixth Line*

People will balk at severe restriction, so use it wisely. Does the situation threaten life and limb? Then set harsh limits. Otherwise, temper regulations with reason.

Influencing Others

The empowered person observes how animal handlers must think like their animals in order to guide them effectively, and learns a lesson about influencing others.

Keywords: Direction, persuasion, opinion, suggestion, exhortation, conviction, convincing, inducement, sway, argument

Encourages: Understanding other points of view; looking at a situation from another's perspective; engaging in debate or rhetoric with the intent of changing minds or swaying opinion; savvy and ethical marketing; making speeches; writing articles

Cautions against: Manipulating others; suppressing meaningful dialogue; attempting to sway public opinion with slanted news or distorted facts; making a game of convincing others of the rightness of your views; deceiving others; speaking with insincerity

THOUGHT QUESTIONS

How firmly do I believe in what I'm preaching or doing?

How do others think and feel about my situation or subject?

What critical evidence helped me change my mind or amend my viewpoint?

What motivates my need to convince others to accept my point of view?

Commentary

Before you attempt to influence others, you should take a long look at your own character and motivations. Why is it important for you to persuade someone to come around to your point of view? Beware selfish impulses; manipulation is the dark side of influence.

When exercised by someone honestly interested in doing what's right and just, influence is a powerful force for good. Wield it boldly, but carefully. Too many people are too easily influenced . . . and when you decide to influence them, you become responsible for their fate.

Love & Relationships

In a relationship, you naturally influence each other. Rather than depend on subterfuge and wheedling, be honest with a partner or friend about what you need. Healthy adults support and enhance each other without depending on manipulation, tricks, or tests.

Work & Projects

Rather than depend exclusively on your own opinions, try getting other points of view. A solution developed in isolation will be far less effective than one created with input from the users. Make sure those with a stake in success play a part in creation.

Guide to Changing Lines

━◯━ *on the First Line*

Stabilize your own spirit before attempting to influence others. Secrets and hidden information will quickly disrupt any attempt to make progress.

━◯━ *on the Second Line*

You can be influenced (and influence others) from a great distance, without realizing it. Your actions have more power than you realize, so act with great caution.

━x━ *on the Third Line*

If you always evaluate yourself in terms of what others think of you, you will live a life of constant turmoil. Get in touch with your own self-worth before proceeding.

━x━ *on the Fourth Line*

You, too, are influenced—mostly by those you hold in awe. Accept their influence with humility . . . but never give up your obligation to find your own path.

━◉━ *on the Fifth Line*

A strong character allows someone in your situation to unify everyone around them. This will unite people in ways that manipulation and deceit never will.

━◉━ *on the Sixth Line*

Talk is, ultimately, just talk. Words will get you so far, and no further. To really influence people, you'll have to take action that generates a change in their lives.

Dealing with Tradition

The empowered person becomes familiar with rules, traditions, and expectations, observing and mindfully transcending them as appropriate.

Keywords: Small points, particulars, fussiness, scrupulousness, meticulousness, micromanagement, fidelity

Encourages: Taking a methodical approach; researching and exhibiting a sensitivity to traditions and cultural restrictions; following the rules; adhering to a plan; honoring forms and rituals with an eye toward their influence on progress and success

Cautions against: Micromanaging a situation; blindly adhering to ritual or tradition; honoring a form or ritual without understanding its significance; being sloppy; rushing through a detailed process; ignoring rules and restrictions

THOUGHT QUESTIONS

How knowledgeable am I with regard to the rules and traditions governing this situation?

When is it time to break the rules? How will I know?

What was the ultimate purpose behind a given rule?

To what extent have I justified stepping outside traditional approaches?

Commentary

Mindless obedience—to law, to tradition, or to religion—is intellectual slavery. The empowered person knows why certain things are done certain ways, and can, as a result, decide whether the letter or the spirit of the law is most important.

An awareness of your mission and duty may lead you to observe very rigorously the laws governing your situation . . . or they may motivate you to step outside what is expected. Before you can adhere to or transcend the details . . . you must be aware of them.

Love & Relationships

Friendships and relationships operate according to rules, and these rules set society's expectations. Should you conform? If you decide to, know why. If you decide to step outside the norm, be prepared to deal graciously with reactions and questions.

Work & Projects

Very likely, any rules or restrictions you encounter have been fabricated to insure the safety of the company and, perhaps secondarily, its employees. Observing them is likely in your favor; build a good case for deviation before stepping outside.

Guide to Changing Lines

▬x▬ *on the First Line*

A certain level of skill, experience, and awareness is needed before stepping out on your own. Embrace tradition as long as possible; you'll wear yourself out opposing it now.

▬x▬ *on the Second Line*

Informed deviation from the rules is often how progress and innovation occur. Be sure you've mastered the forms, though, before setting out to blaze a trail of your own.

▬⊖▬ *on the Third Line*

Self-confidence is no substitute for appropriate caution. Avoid misfortune by becoming more informed and more aware of the rules governing your situation. Take a break.

▬⊖▬ *on the Fourth Line*

Force will lead you, in this case, to misfortune. Be cautious, and most of all, be flexible. Rather than push forward, forge an agreement or link your efforts to those of others.

▬×▬ *on the Fifth Line*

Help is necessary if you desire progress. Go humbly to those with more skill or experience and draw them out. Their achievements hold the key to your success.

▬×▬ *on the Sixth Line*

Pressing forward now will result in overshooting your goals in negative ways. Step back. Observe the forms. Find out more before you continue.

Coasting Along

The empowered person celebrates achievements, but avoids stagnation by quickly setting or revising goals.

Keywords: Lack of momentum, freewheeling, sliding, unhurried, unfocused, meander, ramble, wander, straggle, lack of direction

Encourages: Asking "What's next?"; revisiting your work plan after reaching a milestone; setting purposeful direction; setting your sights on new achievements; moving on; overcoming a fear of defeat or success; overcoming resistance to resuming work

Cautions against: Resting on your laurels; celebrating success to the point that you neglect to make new plans; believing that a moment of achievement will last forever;

causing a setback by avoiding progress; embracing resistance; allowing priorities to be neglected

THOUGHT QUESTIONS

What am I going to achieve now?

How can I make today's milestone into a steppingstone?

To what extent have I defined next steps?

What will the consequences be of not moving on?

Commentary

Following a time of success, everyone deserves a moment to pause and reflect on what's been achieved. But time marches on . . . and so should you. You'll have plenty of time to reminisce over the good old days; for now, the important thing is to take next steps.

Those who fail to set a new course are simply coasting along . . . allowing the situation to dictate their direction. This state of being is especially precarious. Take precautions now. Outline a plan. Envision next steps. Prepare for change—and benefit from it.

Love & Relationships

Chances are, what you're doing today is more a matter of habit than mindful direction. Examine the relationship with an eye toward the future. Where do you need to go? What steps are you taking to get there . . . together?

Work & Projects

Victory is sweet, and a good reputation will take you far. Ultimately, though, you must have an answer to the question: "What have you done lately?" Artists produce art. Writers write. Producers produce. What will you create today? Get started.

Guide to Changing Lines

━●━ on the First Line

Lurching forward is not the same as making progress. You've mistaken activity for direction. Check your goals, define new milestones, and adjust your path.

━x━ on the Second Line

You're depending a bit much on past success and habit. Start a new venture, unfettered by expectations or criticism. Work and wait—new recognition will come.

━●━ on the Third Line

In the name of progress, you may be tempted to send out work or take actions that do not reflect your best effort and highest standards. Resist this strategy; insist on the best.

━x━ on the Fourth Line

You are seeing some signs that something isn't quite right. Go with you gut, and don't let others distract you from these observations. Proceed, but with caution.

━━●━ *on the Fifth Line*

Outward expressions are out of sync with your inner feelings. Work now to bring your actions in line with your thoughts and feelings. Order and success will follow.

━x━ *on the Sixth Line*

You can't go home again, and the "good old days" are in the past. Looking backward is a good way to encourage a nasty fall. Focus on the future instead.

Reaching the Goal

The empowered person observes a fox making his way over a frozen lake, admires his caution and dedication, and resolves to continue making progress.

Keywords: Completion, consummation, fulfillment, finish line, end, accomplishment, milestone, conclusion, termination, achievement, implementation

Encourages: Following though; doing what you need to do to bring a project to completion; taking the final step; bearing up under difficulty or strain; making progress despite the desire to quit; persisting

Cautions against: Blundering forward without a plan; giving up before a milestone is reached; refusing to take new information into account; blinding yourself to alternatives; settling or compromising; failing to fulfill promises or pledges

THOUGHT QUESTIONS

What effort is needed to bring this situation to a close?

How can I keep myself focused on the goal?

How can I find the safest, most efficient path?

What changes in my situation should be taken into account as I strive for success?

Commentary

An experienced fox carefully traverses a frozen lake, stepping lightly and listening for cracks in the ice. A young fox plows ahead blindly—and plunges through. To reach your goal, emulate the old fox: remain alert while making slow and steady progress.

It's especially important not to give up before you get to where you're going. This situation is not yet resolved; you're on the verge of resolution. Giving up now wastes time and effort. Push forward—but attune yourself carefully to the moment.

Love & Relationships

Effort is the key to progress, but effort must be applied in all the right places . . . otherwise, your effort is wasted. Are you working toward the same goals? Investigation may reveal that one of you is pulling when the other is pushing.

Work & Projects

You're making progress. Remain attuned to feedback, and proceed. Be sure your resources are deployed as wisely as possible, and keep an ear to the ground to listen for changes. Make sure everyone is "singing from the same page," as they say.

Guide to Changing Lines

━x━ *on the First Line*

With progress being made, you'll be tempted to dash forward. Don't. A lunge to the finish line won't provide you with the result you seek. Slow and steady wins this race.

━o━ *on the Second Line*

You're right—action is needed, but not at this moment. Watch. Wait. Build your skill or collect more information. Very shortly, this strategy will pay off with great results.

━x━ *on the Third Line*

A time of transition has arrived, but you aren't positioned to take best advantage of it. Create a new situation by appealing to helpers and mentors, then move on.

━o━ *on the Fourth Line*

Completing things will be a struggle! Silence any wavering, and prepare to fight for what you believe in. You'll succeed . . . but you'll have to make a stand in order to do so.

━x━ *on the Fifth Line*

You're overcoming obstacles and uncertainty, and your influence and success is on the rise. Prepare for a degree of success that outshines your previous accomplishments.

━●━ *on the Sixth Line*

Anticipating success, you and your friends may begin planning a celebration. This is natural . . . just don't let things get out of hand and disrupt your final progress.

Appendix A

Hexagram Table

Upper Trigrams

	☰	☳	☵	☶	☷	☴	☲	☱
☰	1	34	5	26	11	9	14	43
☳	25	51	3	27	24	42	21	17
☵	6	40	29	4	7	59	64	47
☶	33	62	39	52	15	53	56	31
☷	12	16	8	23	2	20	35	45
☴	44	32	48	18	46	57	50	28
☲	13	55	63	22	36	37	30	49
☱	10	54	60	41	19	61	38	58

Lower Trigrams

Recommended Reading

I Ching for Beginners presents an extremely simplified oracle inspired by the Book of Changes. With time, you may want to work with an actual translation of the I Ching and explore the unique imagery and depth of the original text.

When that time comes, you may find these resources helpful:

Balkin, Jack M. *The Laws of Change: I Ching and the Philosophy of Life*. New York: Shocken Books, 2002.

Benson, Robert G., ed. *I Ching for a New Age: The Book of Answers for Changing Times*. Garden City Park, NY: Square One Publishers, 2002.

Brennan, J. H. *The Magical I Ching*. St. Paul: Llewellyn Publications, 2000.

Buckland, Raymond. *Coin Divination: Pocket Fortuneteller.* St. Paul: Llewellyn Publications, 2000.

Craze, Richard. *I Ching Book and Card Pack.* Card deck and book. New York: Sterling Publishing, 2000.

Dening, Sarah. *The Everyday I Ching.* New York: St. Martin's Press, 1997.

Iki, Paul. *Yi-King: Tarot Oriental de Paul Iki (I Ching: Oriental Tarot by Paul Iki).* Card deck with companion booklet. Paris: France Cartes, 1978.

Karcher, Stephen, trans. *I Ching: The Classic Chinese Oracle of Change.* London: Vega Books, 2002.

Karcher, Stephen. *Total I Ching: Myths for Change.* London: Time Warner Books, 2003.

Lau, Kwan. *I Ching Tarot.* Card deck and companion book. Trumbull, CT: Weatherhill, Inc., 1996.

Padma, Ma Deva. *Tao Oracle: An Illuminated New Approach to the I Ching.* Card deck and companion book. New York: St. Martin's Press, 2002.

Wilhelm, Richard and Cary F. Baynes. *The I Ching or Book of Changes.* New York: Princeton University Press, 1997.

Free Catalog

Get the latest
information on our
body, mind, and spirit products!
To receive a **free** copy of Llewellyn's consumer
catalog, *New Worlds of Mind & Spirit,* simply
call 1-877-NEW-WRLD or visit our website at
www.llewellyn.com and click on *New Worlds.*

LLEWELLYN ORDERING INFORMATION

Order Online:
Visit our website at www.llewellyn.com, select your books, and order
them on our secure server.

Order by Phone:
- Call toll-free within the U.S. at 1-877-NEW-WRLD
  (1-877-639-9753). Call toll-free within Canada at
  1-866-NEW-WRLD (1-866-639-9753)
- We accept VISA, MasterCard, and American Express

Order by Mail:
Send the full price of your order (MN residents add 6.5% sales tax) in
U.S. funds, plus postage & handling to:

> **Llewellyn Worldwide**
> **2143 Wooddale Drive, Dept. 978-0-7387-0744-0**
> **Woodbury, MN 55125-2989**

Postage & Handling:

Standard (U.S., Mexico, & Canada). If your order is:
$24.99 and under, add $3.00
$25.00 and over, FREE STANDARD SHIPPING

AK, HI, PR: $15.00 for one book plus $1.00 for
each additional book.

International Orders (airmail only):
$16.00 for one book plus $3.00 for each additional book

Orders are processed within 2 business days.
Please allow for normal shipping time. Postage and handling rates subject to change.

The Bright Idea Deck
MARK MCELROY
ILLUSTRATIONS BY ERIC HOTZ

Stumped for a solution to a problem at work? Lacking inspiration for an upcoming project? Experiencing writer's block? *The Bright Idea Deck* is the perfect tool for supercharging the brainstorming process and getting the creative juices flowing.

Designed to generate ideas, expand creative expression, and stimulate thought processes, this brainstorming companion is ideal for the workplace. Filled with colorful, contemporary imagery, this modern Tarot deck suggests hundreds of possible strategies, perspectives, opportunities, motivations, goals, actions, and answers. The boxed kit includes a companion book that describes the deck's structure and card meanings, along with sample scenarios that demonstrate how to use this effective idea generator.

0-7387-0595-0
Boxed kit includes 216-page book, 78-card deck $19.95

What's in the Cards for You?
Test the Tarot

Mark McElroy

Modern society still harbors outdated notions about the tarot, associating it with fortune-telling scam artists, slumber party hijinx, or what they've seen in movies. With good-natured humor and charm, Mark McElroy acknowledges these misconceptions and offers skeptics a hands-on approach to learning the true benefits of tarot.

No dry lectures on tarot history and symbolism will be found here. Instead, McElroy engages readers with thirty fun and practical exercises for exploring the power and utility of tarot. These easy activities take only fifteen minutes each and illustrate the many applications of tarot as a tool for self-understanding, relationship insight, dream analysis, brainstorming, writing inspiration, meditation, problem-solving, and making difficult decisions.

0-7387-0702-3
192 pp., 7½ x 9⅛, illus.   **$14.95**

Taking the Tarot to Heart
Fun & Creative Ways to Improve Your Love Life

MARK McELROY

Waiting for Prince Charming may not be an effective strategy for finding love, just as ignoring relationship problems isn't always the best solution. Instead of letting chance rule romance, Mark McElroy suggests using the Tarot to improve your love life.

No knowledge of the Tarot or belief in the supernatural is necessary. Anyone can use *Taking the Tarot to Heart* to take charge of their romantic destiny. For both singles and couples, this book provides Tarot spreads and exercises to answer questions like "How can I find my soulmate?" and "How can I spice up my love life?" Emphasizing the practical, not the mystical, McElroy demonstrates how easy it is to find creative solutions to relationship issues without bleeding the mystery and meaning out of romance. Many topics are covered: defining your perfect partner, dating, gifts, breakups, granting forgiveness, and more.

0-7387-0536-5
264 pp., 7½ x 9⅛, illus. $16.95

To order, call 1-877-NEW-WRLD
Prices subject to change without notice